Technical Foundations
for Measuring Ego Development
The Washington University
Sentence Completion Test

The LEA Series in
Personality and Clinical Psychology
Irving B. Weiner, Editor

Technical Foundations
for Measuring Ego Development

The Washington University
Sentence Completion Test

Edited by

Jane Loevinger
Washington University

Psychology Press
Taylor & Francis Group

New York   London

First published by Lawrence Erlbaum Associates, Inc. Publishers
10 Industrial Avenue
Mahwah, New Jersey 07430

Reprinted 2008 by Psychology Press

Psychology Press
Taylor & Francis Group
27 Church Road
Hove, East Sussex BN3 2FA

Library of Congress Cataloging-in-Publication-Data

Technical foundations for measuring ego development:
the Washington University Sentence Completion Test / edited by Jane
Loevinger
      p. cm.
    Includes bibliographical references.
    ISBN 0-8058-2059-0 (pbk. : alk. paper)
    1. Sentence Completion test. I. Loevinger, Jane.
BF698.8.S35T43   1998
155.2'83—dc21   97-43778
                                                                                   CIP

Printed in the United States of America
10 9 8 7 6 5 4 3 2 1

Contents

Acknowledgments

I wish to thank all the investigators using the Sentence Completion test (SCT) who graciously supplied us with their data and permission to use the data in revising the scoring manual:

Dr. Sarah Beaton; Dr. Dorothy Billington; Dr. Michael D'Andrea; Dr. Howard Chandler; Dr. Diane Novy; Dr. Dane Ver Merris, and Dr. Gervase Bushe. I hope they will convey to their hundreds of subjects our gratitude for the evident sincerity in virtually all of their replies.

Dr. George Vaillant is a special case, because he gathered the SCT data but my colleagues scored it for him, and I assumed we had a right to use the scored responses, anonymously of course, for our purpose.

The same holds true for many of our own students, whose data, often their dissertation research, became part of our main sample: Dr. Lawrence D. Cohn; Dr. Gabrielle Israelievitch; Dr. Leslie (Gans) Luchene; Dr. Annie Rogers; and David Patterson.

A research project of the duration and complexity of this one cannot succeed without the able and generous assistance of many hands.

Some able and devoted undergraduate and graduate students have served as research assistants, including Tina Nguyen, Susan Lay, Alison Gaa, Claire Simon, and Miri Goldstein. Doyle Cozadd has been my computer consultant and editorial assistant.

Postdoctoral research associates: Vicki Carlson, Kathryn Bobbitt, Lawrence D. Cohn, and P. Michiel Westenberg have been valuable colleagues in our work.

Dr. Westenberg is also fulfilling the important task of extending the range of the test to children, the obvious place to study development, but not an easy place to study sentence completions.

The first graduate student to take part in the study of women's attitudes, the study that after many years grew into the SCT for ego development, was Dr. Kitty LaPerriere. The imprint of her insights is still visible in this revised scoring manual.

Our longest standing colleague, Dr. Augusto Blasi, came into our work early and is still sustaining us with the breadth of his knowledge and his incisive insights,

My principal debt is to Dr. Vicki Carlson and Dr. Lê Xuân Hy, who, as the table of contents shows, are authors of major chapters. Lê Xuân Hy was responsible for gathering the data and programing it for managing by computer. He also suggested having a chapter on multicultural uses of the SCT. Dr. Carlson has shown the many uses of the SCT in other cultures and other languages, thereby supplying an important kind of validation of the concept and the method. Both Dr. Carlson and Dr. Hy have contributed to this book beyond their own chapters.

—*Jane Loevinger*

CHAPTER 1

History of the Sentence Completion Test (SCT) for Ego Development

Jane Loevinger
Washington University

Prior to the 1950s, most subjects for psychological research in the United States were "normal, White, native-born men," or children. The few studies of girls and women tended to be about the nature and extent of gender differences in intelligence or occasionally other abilities.

In the 1950s and 1960s, several investigators (Loevinger, Sweet, Ossorio, & LaPerriere, 1962; Schaefer & Bell 1958; Sears, Maccoby, & Levin, 1957; Shoben, 1949) more or less independently began studies of women's attitudes toward problems of family life. Evidently it was their function as mothers that finally brought women to the attention of research psychologists. This was the era of mother-blaming (Loevinger, 1953), during which mothers were held accountable for the sins and personal failings of their children; so one might suspect that the implicit purpose of most such studies was to protect or defend the children.

However, our small, informal group (Loevinger et al., 1962) had the explicit aim to study personality patterns of mothers and of women in general. The initial group, all women, all had studied some psychology. Some, but not all, were mothers. The group included one professional clinician, Blanche Sweet; one experimentalist, Marilyn Rigby; and me, a psychometrician. Various other persons seeking part-time work, including some men, met with the group at various times.

We started with a psychometric approach, objective test items administered to several samples of women, with the results analyzed statistically. We were looking for statistically homogeneous clusters of items, as evidence for personality patterns or traits.

Our test, the Family Problems scale, began with a pool of items covering all the problems of family life throughout the day and throughout the life cycle, that we could think of. Although the initial focus was on problems of family life, there was always the larger aim to learn about personality more broadly. In addition to covering the content area broadly, items were included to test various theories about personality, women, and family attitudes, for example, punitiveness versus permissiveness; acceptance versus rejection of the "feminine role," fixation on different psychosexual modes and zones; dependence versus independence; conventional versus flexible gender-role conception; characteristic defense mechanisms, and so on. These were the terms in which clinical psychologists, social workers, and psychoanalysts discussed their clients in that era.

The item format was paired choice, to minimize response sets. Profiting from the findings of the Berkeley studies of the authoritarian personality (Adorno, Frenkel-Brunswik, Levinson, & Sanford, 1950), we attempted to bypass obvious defenses by wording both choices in a socially acceptable manner.

Participants for the initial test tryout were 346 women, obtained from unusually diverse sources, including college student groups; members of various mothers' groups associated with churches and public schools; patients in outpatient clinics; and relatives who accompanied the patients.

Perhaps it was fortunate that none of us had a position where we were tempted to settle for testing a single sophomore psychology class. Our circumstance of being outside academic walls induced us to sample women more broadly, which was also more appropriate to our aims.

Analysis of the test was based on all of the test protocols ($N = 202$), regardless of source, on which all 206 items were answered. To obtain statistical clusters of items, we used the method of homogeneous keying (Loevinger, Gleser, & DuBois, 1953), a quasi-factorial method based on intercorrelations of all items.

Because the original pool of items was drawn more broadly than any statistical cluster that was expected to emerge, the clusters could be characterized by examining the content of items included and those excluded.

The results were surprising. None of the empirical statistical clusters corresponded exactly to any of the theories or conceptions that gave rise to the items. "Acceptance of the feminine role" split into two clusters, one referring to women's biological role, one to their conventional social role, and, moreover, the two clusters were negatively correlated. No cluster corresponded to any of the psychosexual stages posited by psychoanalysis.

The largest cluster of items incorporated much of what was usually called *punitiveness versus permissiveness.* The trouble with that label was that some items having direct reference to punishment, such as, "No child should be permitted to strike his mother," versus "A mother should not be harsh with a small child who hits her" were not included, whereas some items having no reference to punishment, such as, "A father should be his son's best pal," were prominently included.

The characterization of women high on the largest cluster of items (Loevinger et al., 1962) was remarkably similar to that of the "authoritarian personality" (Adorno et al., 1950); in both instances the element of inability to conceptualize inner life played an unexpectedly large part (Loevinger, 1993b). Therefore, the scale built on this cluster of items was called Authoritarian Family Ideology (AFI). This was an unanticipated finding.

Kitty LaPerriere interposed that in her experience in child-guidance clinics whose referrals came from courts and schools, many mothers cannot be described as falling anywhere along a continuum like AFI, ranging from rigid, conventional, and authoritarian to democratic, permissive, and flexible. Instead of being identified with authority, many are antagonistic and resistant to authority; instead of describing themselves or their children with stereotyped, conventional, socially approved banalities, they had almost nothing to say, probably in part out of resistance to authority, but in part out of an inability to conceptualize themselves or their way of life as something to be described, beyond describing diffuse physical discomforts.

Clinical investigation, LaPerriere found, often reveals that such women have chaotic personalities, lead disorganized lives, and are given to primitive impulse gratification. To encompass that group of women in the continuum, we had to recognize that authoritarianism was not its extreme but a midpoint.

This recognition required a sea change; instead of looking for traits or traitlike variables that were linear or bipolar continua, we defined our variable in terms of a milestone sequence, with qualitatively different markers along its developmental course.

To study AFI a stratified, more or less representative sample of women was drawn from postpartum patients in St. Louis area maternity wards. AFI was shown to be unrelated to religion (Catholic, Protestant, or Jewish), to be strongly related to education (ranging from part high school to college graduate), and to be significantly related to experience in childrearing, as measured by parity, primiparous mothers versus those having their second or third child. A significant relation to education and parity remained even when age was held constant by covariance analysis. These results suggested that AFI measured a developmental variable.

At this point, LaPerriere's faculty advisor, Abel Ossorio, suggested that what we were measuring as AFI encompassed so much, including the wide range of content in the items of AFI, that no term less broad than *ego development* sufficed. AFI encompassed aspects of moral development, interpersonal relations, and conceptual complexity.

Although LaPerriere warned us that the term *ego development* was used somewhat differently by psychoanalysts, it seemed to carry the meaning of what we were measuring better than any alternative. Anyhow, Freud did not use the term, *ego* (Loevinger, 1976, p. 4).

The facts that the Berkeley studies (Adorno et al., 1950) focused primarily on political life and that their samples were mostly male, contrasting with our female samples and focus on small scale domestic concerns, strengthened the impression that the variable being measured was of central importance in personality. As always happens with a new conception, there was no established test to validate our interpretation. We therefore chose to look at its network of relations with other variables, beginning with a semiprojective test of sentence completions. The sentence completion technique is one of the oldest devices in differential psychology. Many sentence completion tests had been used widely in psychology, but none of them had a scoring manual for our variable and our interpretation. Moreover, although the methods for constructing objective tests have been thoroughly worked out, there were no established methods for constructing scoring manuals for projective tests. Thus, our next major task was to develop a methodology for constructing a sentence completion scoring manual to serve our purpose.

At this point, Elizabeth J. Nettles began to study problems of adolescent girls and young women, in terms of their acceptance of their biological and social roles and relationships with their mothers. Nettles adapted some sentence stems from previous SCTs, and added other stems germane to her interests. Although her original research project was not completed, the sentence completion method proved so interesting and so fruitful, that work with her SCT (Form 9-62) continued.

Theoretical guidelines for scoring the test were found in the conception of interpersonal maturity and interpersonal integration (I-level) described by C. Sullivan, Grant (later Warren), and Grant (1957), who had also used an SCT of their own devising. Although their conception took shape in the study of young male delinquents, in broad outline it fit our data, again a confirmation of the general importance of the variable we had come on. One of their co-workers, Virginia Ives (Word), joined our research group at this time. She brought to us a rich store of their findings as applied to the SCT, findings that had not been fully set down in print.

We began by adopting four of their stages as a scale: roughly the Impulsive stage (I-2, now E-2), the Conformist stage (I-3, now E-4), the Conscientious Stage (I-4, now E-6), and the Autonomous stage (I-5, now E-8).

Our raters said an intermediate stage was needed between the Impulsive and the Conformist stages. The I-level system had an opportunistic subgroup of the Conformist stage that was called "I-3-cons"; but there were few blatant expressions of opportunism among the girls and women who were the usual subjects in our studies. The term *cons* did not fit any of them.

We therefore adopted the code term *Delta* (now E-3),and its corresponding concept from Kenneth Isaacs' (1956) system of *interpersonal relatedness* for the stage between impulsive and conformist. Isaacs' system is similar to that of C. Sullivan, Grant, and Grant, but has more fully elaborated the conception of an opportunistic stage between the impulsive and the conformist ones (Loevinger 1976; see Table 1.1).

TABLE 1.1

Some Characteristics of Stages of Ego Development: I-Levels and E-Levels

		Characteristics		
Level	Code	Impulse Control	Interpersonal Mode	Conscious Preoccupation
Impulsive	E2 (I-2)	Impulsive	Egocentric, dependent	Bodily feelings
Self-Protective	E3 (Delta)	Opportunistic	Manipulative, wary	"Trouble," control
Conformist	E4 (I-3)	Respect for rules	Cooperative, loyal	Appearances, behavior
Self-Aware	E5 (I-3/4)	Exceptions allowable	Helpful, self-aware	Feelings, problems, adjustment
Conscientious	E6 (I-4)	Self-evaluated standards, self-critical	Intense, responsible	Motives, traits, achievements
Individualistic	E7 (I-4/5)	Tolerant	Mutual	Individuality, development, roles
Autonomous	E8 (I-5)	Coping with conflict	Interdependent	Self-fulfillment, psychological causation
Integrated	E9 (I-6)		Cherishing individuality	Identity

Note. The code for the previous version used I-levels and Delta; the current code uses E-levels. Adapted from Loevinger (1976, 1987).

FORMS OF SCT MANUALS

Because we initially had no scoring manual, we discussed as a group how to classify each completion, trying to imagine the person who would give such a response. A set of these classified responses was assembled as the first tentative scoring manual. For each sentence stem it gave examples at each stage, to the extent that the test protocols on hand permitted. Thus, it was an *exemplar manual*. Most projective techniques have exemplar scoring manuals. As soon as we tried to use this manual for a new set of responses by different subjects, it became evident that it did not offer adequate guidance for raters, because it did not show why any example was given its particular rating.

The next step was to group the examples into categories, with category titles chosen to help the rater see why those responses belonged at that level. That resulted in a *categorized manual*. People of different levels, as judged by their total protocols, often wrote about the same or very similar content. Thus, the category title cannot just name the content. To distinguish levels we had to observe fine differences in the terms of their responses.

The research group (at that time Kitty LaPerriere, Virginia Ives Word, Elizabeth Nettles, Nina Gach deCharms, Augusto Blasi, and me) was more confident in judging the ego level of a total protocol than that of a single response out of context. Additional considerations are admissible when judging a total protocol that are not available when rating a single response. Repetition of a simple, pat, cliché-like phrase for several items suggests a low-level protocol. Richness and variety of the 36 responses suggests a high level. Inclusion of several different high-level themes, such as conceptual complexity, personality as developing, and psychological causation, was considered as stronger evidence of high ego level than several mentions of a single one of those themes. With a categorized manual it became possible to verify or disconfirm judgments incorporated in the categories, by use of total protocol ratings (TPRs). This internal consistency method became the basis for all further refinements of the manual.

MICROVALIDATION OF THE MANUAL

The empirical verification method was as follows: A fairly large and heterogeneous sample was scored by the then current manual, recording the category as well as the level of each response to each item.

For each item in the test, separately, all responses in each category were listed with the TPR of the protocol on which that response occurred in the sample, in order of TPR. Then this sheet, called a *decoding sheet*, would be examined for possible improvements in the manual. It was rarely the case that all the TPRs for a category were the same, just as it rarely happened that all the items on a given person's test protocol had the same rating. That is the expected *décalage*.

Sometimes raters did not interpret a category in the intended manner; In that case a better name was found for the category, or better examples were chosen for the next revision of the manual.

A category could be moved to a higher or lower level, or it could be split into two parts, each part going to a different level. Using the mean or mode of the TPRs was not suitable as a method of deciding where a category belonged; it was necessary to take into account the base rates of TPRs in the sample being used. Otherwise, if most of the protocols in a sample were Conformist, almost all the categories would seem to belong at that level.

The final form of the manual was a *rationalized category manual*, attempting to explain theoretically why each category was placed at the level it was. Although complete rationalization of every decision could not be accomplished, the aim gave direction to our endeavor, and tied it to the larger aim of providing insight into personality development generally. It was that larger aim that ruled out the obvious psychometric method of simply maximizing prediction of the TPRs.

Ground Rules

The ground rules for construction and use of the manual were that every example given in the manual was a response that someone had really given; there were no invented examples.

Every response had to be rated, even responses that appeared intuitively not to be relevant to ego level.

A default rating was needed for omissions and completely incoherent or otherwise unratable responses; Conformist (I-3, now E-4) was the default rating, because almost every protocol, regardless of level, had some conformist ratings; so that rating on a few items would not preclude any TPR.

Item responses were rated first out of context, that is, without reference to any data about the subject (except gender, female in all of our early studies), and without reference to other responses by the subject.

The rater was directed to consider each response at the minimal inferential level, that is, to look for what the subject herself regarded as the meaning or import of her response, not for unconscious or hidden meanings. In other words, to read the response at the level at which people give account of their thoughts, actions, and motives to themselves.

The language of the manual was plain English; inferential or technical terms such as *superego* or *defense mechanism*, or *ego* were not used in the manual.

Although the reason for rating every response was psychometric, so that every protocol would have the same number of ratings, this rule had the effect of constantly testing our intuitions, and it led to substantive findings.

Initially, it was assumed that humorous remarks or derogatory remarks about the test itself, would not be ratable. Our experience showed, on the contrary, that hostile humor, particularly when directed at the test or the tester, was a reliable clue to low level, usually Delta (now E-3). On the other hand, a benign, existential humor was sometimes found on very high level protocols.

Some psychologists, doing content analyses for various purposes, consider clichés unratable, but we found that they are clues to conformity.

There was a long period of mini-experiments, for example, trying different sentence stems, different arrangements of items, different lengths of the test.

Gradually, the test settled to 36 stems as the optimal number to get an adequate picture of the subject's response repertoire without boring her or taxing her patience to the point where she refused to answer. (Later it was learned that several other SCTs use between 30 and 40 items.)

One small study in which about a dozen raters each rated every item showed that each rater arrived at a different number of omissions for many protocols. Thus, we learned that special care was needed to specify rating of ambiguous responses, such as, for example, "?".

No basis was found for interpreting omissions in terms of the apparent topic of the sentence stem. However, a considerable number of omissions was more characteristic of low-level protocols, than of median or high-level ones. Items frequently omitted were candidates for deletion in subsequent revisions of the SCT.

Manual Samples Not Normative. The fact that the test was being used in many small, sometimes informal, studies helped its evolution. However, there were never any norms, although some later investigators have erroneously referred to the manual as if it embodied a normative sample (perhaps to spare themselves the trouble of assembling an appropriate comparison sample for their own study).The manual necessarily eliminated repeated responses; if there were not many such, the project would be unworkable.

The samples came widely from the social spectrum, but they were all opportunistic samples, not systematically representative of any population. For example, Virginia Turner tested applicants for The George Warren Brown School of Social Work of Washington University, St. Louis, because it was a group she was interested in and would work with. Other samples were obtained similarly, because students or colleagues wanted to use the SCT in their own studies.

Over a period of time, raters began to use intermediate or "transitional" ratings between the stages with which we started. The most important transitional rating was that between Conformist and Conscientious, because that is where many people are.

Although there were attempts to identify characteristics of transitional levels per se, as contrasted with "stages," none were fruitful. The designation as stage or as transition remained arbitrary.

Ultimately, it was appreciated that the scoring manual had evolved to a point where other researchers would find it useful. The skills developed in many rating groups in psychology, such as the Berkeley studies of the authoritarian personality (Adorno et al., 1950), were lost when the group disbanded.

To prevent that from happening to our work, a rule was made that everything had to be written down, including instructions to typists. That rule is hard to hold to, but any lapse was later regretted.

Freezing and Evaluating the Manual.   In order to evaluate the manual, we had to stop experimenting and settle on a version to evaluate. It was called the *prepublication manual.*

Then an entirely new sample of subjects was drawn, called the *sealed sample,* because none of the prospective raters saw any of the protocols until time to do their rating.

Typists prepared test copies and item response lists for each item, using a meticulous coding system, so that different responses from a given protocol would not have the same number, to ensure that each item was rated independently of the others. This was accomplished by gifted and heroically conscientious secretaries, but it is now possible by computerized spread sheets (chapter 6). Careful decoding was necessary when ratings were completed, in order to determine the item ogive for each subject, to evaluate interrater agreement, test homogeneity, and item validities (i.e., correlations with TPR). These methods and the subsequent data analyses of the sealed sample were the responsibility of Ruth Wessler.

When the prepublication manual was completed, two senior raters, Blasi and I went over all responses to all items, one stage at a time. On the basis of our impressions, the characterizations of the stages changed somewhat. The major change was that the Opportunistic stage, Delta, was renamed Self-Protective, because there were rarely outright expressions of opportunism in our subjects.

Above the Autonomous stage a higher stage was tentatively identified as Integrated. Some transitional or intermediate levels were sketched. The most important was the transition from Conformist to Conscientious. It was first called Self-Aware, then called Conscientious-Conformist; currently it is again called Self-Aware (E-5).

Determining TPRs

The prepublication manual contained instructions for how to rate each of the 36 items. There remained the problem of the TPR, the scoring algorithm for the total protocol.

Averaging the item ratings was considered, but it would lead to almost no extreme TPRs, and would certainly underestimate the importance of intuitively convincing extreme responses.

The modal item rating was a possibility, but for the sealed sample, that rule placed three quarters of the participants at the Conformist level and the remaining one quarter at the Conscientious level.

An appealing idea was to look at the profile (distribution) of item response ratings for each protocol, comparing it to typical item profiles of the best examples of protocols judged to be at each of the several stages. In principle, that seemed a good idea, but it has the fatal flaw that a large number of parameters would be required to make each distinction between pairs of adjacent levels.

This consideration led to a unique algorithm, the *ogive rules,* based on the cumulative distribution of item ratings for a protocol. A single parameter then suffices for distinguishing between every pair of adjacent TPRs.

An alternative method of evaluating the TPR is the Item Sum Score (ISS). This requires translating the item ratings to an ordinal scale and adding.

There are two problems with the ISS. In order to get a stage score for the total protocol, one must translate back; parameters must be set using a large sample for which ogive TPRs are available or intuitive TPRs have been agreed on by experts. The more serious problem for the ISS is that different investigators using the SCT have felt free to renumber our stages and then to translate their item ratings into their own ad hoc ordinal scale, which is not comparable to ours or to those of other studies based on different ad hoc numbering systems. The new E-level code is meant to end this confusing practice, because it is also an ordinal scale.

Under some circumstances comparisons can use the numerical item sum itself. Examples where the ISS would be appropriate are studies with designs calling for pretest compared to posttest, or experimental group compared to control group. Because the ISS depends on 36 separate item ratings, and, given the item ratings, does not require judgment, it is probably more reliable than ogive TPRs, especially for beginners.

Data from ratings of the sealed sample showed that the manual was ready for publication. Interrater reliability was excellent, about .90 both for items and TPRs.

Internal consistency, was shown by the coefficient alpha of .90. Principal component analysis showed that there was only one appreciable factor or component in the item ratings (analyses of Ruth Wessler).

THE PRACTICE EXERCISES

To test the completeness of our written instructions and practice exercises, some new untrained raters were given no instructions except those written down in the manual (including prescribed practice exercises), and they were not permitted to discuss doubtful points until they had completed their assignments of rating portions of the sealed sample. Their ratings agreed as well with those of previously trained, experienced raters as the latter agreed with each other.

That experiment proved that we had accomplished the objective of providing new raters with adequate training exercises. Provision of training exercises for raters is probably unique to the SCT among projective test manuals.

The published manual differs from the prepublication version only by minor corrections resulting from feedback from the extensive study of the sealed sample.

The most distinctive and crucially valuable feature of our method of manual construction is the microvalidation of manual categories by repeated cycling, applying the manual to a new sample, "decoding" the ratings to see how well the parts of the manual are doing, and making indicated minor changes before applying the manual again.

By this method the descriptions of the several stages were shaped by the data, and our conception of ego development took shape.

The methods by which the data were handled to create successive versions of the manual were primarily the work of Ruth Wessler. The published manual (Loevinger, Wessler, & Redmore, 1970) was the result of close collaboration of the three authors.

Chapter 2
Revision of the SCT: Creating Form 81

Jane Loevinger
Washington University
Lawrence D. Cohn
University of Texas at El Paso

The SCT was originally devised as part of a program of research on women's attitudes and personalities, and the particular study it was first intended for concerned women's and adolescent girls' "acceptance of the feminine (or woman's) role," a topic that now sounds dated. This interest led to inclusion of some sentence stems (e.g., "A woman's body—," and "A pregnant woman—") (SCT for women, Form 9-62) which lacked face validity in use of the test with men. In further research, a parallel test for men was needed. The SCT devised for men included many of the original items but deleted those that seemed most inappropriate and added an equal number of stems that tapped topics more acceptable to men (SCT for men form 9-62 for men, Appendix C).

Over the years, piecemeal modifications of the SCT were made by various of our co-workers, to meet the needs of particular projects. Supplementary manuals for new items and for use with male samples were created by Redmore, Loevinger, and Tamashiro (1978–1981) and by Hy and Loevinger (1989), but they were not published, because it was always intended that they would be supplanted by carefully researched manuals, like those in the present revision.

As use of the test with men and adolescent boys increased, and as interest in gender differences was renewed, the original forms of the SCT presented problems: The forms for men and women were not closely comparable; the question remained whether item content was still more appropriate for women; and for the most comparable items the scoring manuals used for men were derived originally for use with women.

We therefore decided to create definitive new forms of the SCT to meet as far as possible those problems (Loevinger, 1985), using as guidance the data accumulated, mainly with Forms 11-68 for men and women, scored using the 1970 manual and the supplementary manuals as available. We began by setting up clear criteria for what we wanted the new forms to do and be.

CRITERIA FOR REVISING THE SCT

Close Comparability of Forms for Men and Women. Forms for men and women cannot be made exactly the same without sacrificing richness of content. What, for instance, is the male equivalent of "The worst thing about being a woman—," or "Sometimes she wished that—," or "A good mother—" ? In matching the two forms we sometimes changed the noun ("The worst thing about being a man—"); sometimes changed the pronoun ("Sometimes he wished that—"); and sometimes repeated the content ("A good father—" and "A good mother—" on both the form for men and that for women).

Interesting and Varied Content. This criterion limits carrying out the first one. Repeated content leads some people to repeat answers. For example, in response to "Men are lucky because—" some people say "see answer to No. 12," referring to their previous answer to "Women are lucky because—." Those two stems have both been retained, because they usually elicit interesting and different answers. But frequent use of parallel stems would alienate many subjects and lead to impoverished protocols.

The women's form formerly in most frequent use, Form 11-68, had five stems with the word *mother* in them; three were dropped.

First and Second Pages Usable as Abbreviated Alternate Forms. The 36-item form is recommended for virtually all uses, because that appears to be about the optimal length, balancing the need for breadth and reliability against the subjects' toleration for the task. (Several SCTs of other authors have between 30 and 40 items.) Furthermore, all psychometric data in our varied studies have been gathered with forms of that length.

Because there is much overlap of content with older forms and because items are more or less equivalent as measures, data gathered with previous forms remain applicable to the new 36-item forms.

Many investigators demand shorter forms on the probably mistaken belief that an appreciable amount of subjects' time is saved. By the time a person has found her or his pencil and settled down to the task, only a small amount of time is taken by the additional items.

However, where there is need for a pre- and posttest or for forms given under two conditions, the two pages are usable as equivalent forms. All stems on the first page are identical for men and women. Item content on the two pages is similar. Many researchers have been using a "12-item short form" (Holt, 1980), which unfortunately was a random selection of items from previous versions; some of the items on the 12-item form have never had a research-based item manual; it is therefore particularly unsuitable for new users, who are those most likely to use it. This 12-item form was put together by a survey researcher who had no training in the SCT. The new 18-item forms should replace the 12-item form when a short form is needed.

Selection of Some Items Originally Composed for Men and for Which the Scoring Manuals Were Derived From Male Protocols. " R u l e s are—" is the only item whose original manual was based on a sample comprising both men and women.

In choosing between the two stems, "When I get mad—" and "When I am criticized—," which are about equally good and draw similar responses, the latter was chosen because it had a manual derived from male samples.

Other items constructed to have face validity for men include "A man's job—" and "Crime and delinquency could be halted if—."

Manuals for "A husband has a right to—" and "A good father—" were made with men's responses, although the latter was partially guided by a prior manual for "A good mother—." Thus, the 1981 test form partially balances the use for men of stems originally devised for women with the use for women of stems originally devised for men.

Selection of the Most Valid Items. As all items proved to have satisfactory validity (i.e., item-total correlation), the lowest being .40 for women and .32 for men, this criterion was weighted least. The stem "I am—" was retained despite relatively low validity because it differs from other items and provides at least some comparison with the "Who Am I" technique.

"My husband and I will—" was dropped despite high validity, even without a manual, because widows, divorcees, and some single women found it objectionable.

Avoidance of Successions of Items That Suggest Connected Answers. In the previous form for men, the stem "My father—" was followed by three stems in which the pronoun *he* occurred. Many men took this to mean that those three items were to be answered with respect to their fathers.

The standard rating procedure calls for rating each response out of context. Out-of-context rating is made difficult by connected answers.

The First Item on Each Page Sufficiently Structured to be Relatively Easy to Complete.   Various items have been used as the initial one in past forms. "The thing I like about myself is—" led to too much self-consciousness when it was the initial item.

When "Education—" occurs at or near the beginning of the test, it is likely to be answered by a factual report, such as "finished high school."

"Raising a family—-" once seemed like a neutral starting item, but now may be responded to as if it were a put-down, particularly by women with serious career aims. (We noted this particularly because one of our samples included women in an engineering college.)

The Last Item on Each Page Should Not Encourage Hostile or Self-Derogatory Completions.   If such items are last, they may leave respondents uncomfortable.

Limiting all these considerations to some extent, the aim was to retain as much of the content and format of the previous form as possible, particularly the women's Form 11-68, because it had proved fruitful in past studies.

ALTERATION OF SCT FOR SPECIFIC GROUPS

There is no objection in principle to a researcher substituting one or a few stems of his or her own choosing for an equal number of stems in the new Form 81. That might be done because for some reason the given content was deemed objectionable to a group or because some other content was of particular interest in a study.

In such cases, all of the criteria here are applicable. A new item will almost certainly not be scored as validly as the deleted item; and an unpropitious order may even compromise the validity of remaining items.

Considering the years of experience that were required to evolve Form 81, the likelihood of changing the test for the worse seems greater than the chance for improvement. We have virtually never had objections to the content of the stems from subjects who were given the test.

Occasionally objections were voiced by gatekeepers, that is, principals, whose permission was needed to test school children; or obstreticians, whose permission was needed to gain access to postpartum women in hospital. In view of relaxation of public standards for what can be talked about, that problem is unlikely to be a large one.

Form 77 for boys and Form 77 for girls (see Appendix C) were made somewhat comparable using some but not all of the principles just listed. There are no short forms for them. The girls' Form 77 has 27 items in common with Form 81 for women, the boys' Form 77 has 26 items in common with Form 81 for men (Table 2.3).

EVALUATION OF THE ITEMS

Method

The data used to evaluate the items came from 454 men and 350 women, all tested using Form 11-68 for men or Form 11-68 for women, all tested for the first time and under standard instructions.

The tests were scored in three large composite samples in the years 1976, 1977, and 1978. Each composite sample incorporated subsamples from a variety of studies available for rating at that time. The cases were coded and intermixed so that raters did not know what subsample a given response or protocol came from. (Incidentally, that is a practice we recommend wherever possible.)

Subjects included college students from several colleges, ranging from freshmen to graduate students; husbands and wives taking part in marital counseling, (obtained from a variety of sources) together with their matched control subjects of husbands and wives not in counseling; mothers and fathers of senior students in a racially mixed public high school of an inner suburb; inmates in a federal penitentiary; and parents taking part in counseling for child neglect or abuse. The socioeconomic and age range was great for both men and women, but overweighted with college students.

Items were rated by trained and experienced raters using the 1970 manual and then current supplementary manuals (Redmore et al., 1978–1981). A few items for which no manual existed were rated using general knowledge of the test. Every final rating was based on at least two independent ratings.

Results

Table 2.1 shows the distribution of ego level for the total of all samples used in this study, by gender. (Neither this nor any other of our studies purports to give normative data.) For both men and women, the median lies between the Self-Aware and the Conscientious stages. The women have a median rating marginally higher than the men; however, with the exception of the spouse study (Nettles & Loevin-

TABLE 2.1

Distribution of E-Levels, by Gender, Composite Sample for Evaluating Items

Level	Code	Women				Men				%	
		Years				Years					
		76	77	78	Total	76	77	78	Total	W	M
Integrated	9	2	5		7		3	1	4	2.0	.9
Autonomous	8	11	12	2	25	9	3	2	14	7.1	3.6
Individualistic	7	25	17	13	55	21	25	12	58	15.7	12.8
Conscientious	6	57	58	21	136	101	51	41	193	38.9	42.5
Conscientious-Conformist	5	25	49	10	84	68	27	31	126	24.0	27.8
Conformist	4	8	12	1	21	17	11	6	34	6.0	7.5
Delta-3*		3	5		8	6	5	2	13	2.3	2.9
Self-Protective	3	1	7		8	8			8	2.3	1.8
E2/Delta*		1	2		3	1			1	.9	.2
Impulsive	2		3		3	3			3	.9	.7

Note. Modified from Table 2, p. 424, of Rev SCT

*Now obsolete

TABLE 2.2

Validity of Different Forms of Items, by Gender

	Form 11-68, Women		Form 11-68, Men		Form 81, Both
Stem Content	N	Median	N	Median	N
First person	16	.50	14	.425	13
Third person	4	.455	6	.40	3
Impersonal (common noun)	16	.495	16	.475	20

ger, 1983), the male and female samples are not matched. For the spouse study, the mean ego levels for men and women are identical. In the total sample (sum of the three composite samples), the women also have a greater dispersion in total protocol rating (TPR; 1.46 compared to 1.25 for men).

Overall, the items are more valid (i.e., predictive of TPR) for women than for men; however, if the difference in dispersion of TPRs is corrected for, there is no difference (actually, a minimal difference favoring men).

Looking at item content, the stems can be classed as first person ("My father—," and "When they talked about sex, I—"); third person ("Sometimes she wished that—," and "Usually he felt that sex—"); and common noun or impersonal ("A good father—," and "Being with other people—").

This classification refers only to the stems, not the actual or usual answers. The median validity of the first-person and impersonal items is the same for women, but for men impersonal stems are more valid (Table 2.2). Third-person stems are on average less valid for both men and women.

Form 81 has more impersonal stems, as compared with previous forms of the SCT, at the expense of both third-person and first-person stems. Presumably, that will make the SCT more favorable for men.

Considering the origin of this SCT in studies about women conducted mostly by women investigators, making the test more favorable for men was an appropriate consideration.

Table 2.3 (see p. 18) presents the validity (item-total correlation) of all the items retained in Form 81, as determined by the foregoing research using Form 11-68. Most of the data were gathered in studies supervised by Redmore. Statistical analyses for Table 2.3 were done by Cohn.

TABLE 2.3

Validity(Item-TPR Correlations) of Items Retained in Form 81

Stem	Validity		Form 77
	Women	Men	
1 When a child will not join in group activities	.57	.48	G, B
2 Raising a family	.50	.47	G, B
3 When I am criticized		.45	G, B
4 A man's job		.45	B
5 Being with other people	.48	.53	G, B
6 The thing I like about myself is	.42	.43	G, B
7 My mother and I	.50		G
8 What gets me into trouble is	.50	.41	G, B
9 Education	.56	.56	G, B
10 When people are helpless	.49	.44	G, B
11 Women are lucky because	.40	.46	G, B
12 A good father		.50	B
13 A girl has a right to	.47		G
14 When they talked about sex, I	.57	.40	
15 A wife should	.56	.51	G
16 I feel sorry	.53	.52	G, B
17 A man feels good when		.46	
18 Rules are	.52	.50	G, B
19 Crime and delinquency could be halted if		.43	G, B
20 Men are lucky because	.47	.42	G, B
21 I just can't stand people who		.43	G, B
22 At times she (he) worried about	.46	.38	G, B
23 I am	.40		G, B
24 A woman feels good when	.43		G, B
25 My main problem is	.59	.42	G, B
26 A husband has a right to		.47	B
27 The worst thing about being a woman (man)	.53	.52	G, B
28 A good mother	.51		G
29 When I am with a man (woman)	.54	.51	
30 Sometimes she (he) wished that	.46	.36	G, B
31 My father	.50		G, B
32 If I can't get what I want	.53	.36	G, B
33 Usually she (he) felt that sex	.45	.39	
34 For a woman a career is	.49		
35 My conscience bothers me if	.46	.46	G, B
36 A woman (man) should always	.50	.49	G, B

Note. Stems for men and women are identical except for those with a word in parentheses.
Validity is item-total correlation obtained using data of Form 11-68.
B indicates item appears in Form 77 for boys; G, Form 77 for girls.
Where no validity is recorded, the item did not appear on the corresponding Form 11-68.
Parenthetical word indicates change used for men's form.

Chapter 3
Revision of the Scoring Manual

Jane Loevinger
Washington University
Lê Xuân Hy
U.S. Government Acounting Office
with assistance of
Kathryn Bobbitt
Private Practice, Waverly, WV

After the SCT had been carefully revised (chapter 2), a new scoring manual covering the new items and based on samples including male as well as female subjects became imperative. The occasion was used also to adopt a new E-level code (see Table 1.1), replacing the patchwork of "I-level" stages, half stages, and transitions (including Delta) partly borrowed from previous writers, partly improvised ad hoc.

Our resources were never adequate to undertake a classical psychometric standardization, using representative samples of the population. However, in comparison with what most projective techniques offer as standardization samples, sometimes no more than a few dozen cases, this has been a major, almost heroic project.

ASSEMBLING THE DATA

First we sent a letter to researchers, mostly psychologists, who had written to our project about using the SCT in their research. We explained our desire to use as many and as disparate subjects as possible in revising the scoring manual. Those who replied were uniformly positive, encouraging the revision and offering to share their data with us. Our research method permitted use of data only from studies that had used the 36-item Form 81 with standard instructions, where the investigators had already scored their protocols and had recorded item ratings, preferably including also the category. That narrowed the field.

By this method several samples were obtained, supplied by researchers from various parts of the country; so these data extended our range of samples. A number of studies by our own students and colleagues had used Form 81, and those samples were also used. Most data arrived on disks, either Macintosh or PC DOS. Different spreadsheet and word processing programs had been used, and the data were arranged in various ways. A major effort put all these data into a common format, a single Excel spreadsheet (one for each item) suitable for further manipulation (see chapter 6).

Internal evidence suggested that the ogive rules, which evidently were inadequately explained in the 1970 manual, had not always been applied correctly. Therefore a computer macro was devised that applied the strict ogive rules to the distribution of item ratings, which at that point had to be assumed to be substantially correct. These macro-derived ogive total protocol ratings (TPRs) were substituted for the investigators' TPRs in all data, including studies done at Washington University by our own students. (Parenthetically, every source of data presented problems that required attention to some individual responses to correct errors that were obviously clerical and were presumably introduced in transcribing the responses or processing them subsequently. A response might be listed as having been given to one item, when it was obviously inappropriate for it but appropriate for the item just before or after.)

The basic group of samples used in manual revision is listed in Table 3.1.

THE MAIN SAMPLE

The sample of available protocols, 1,160 cases, has more women than men. In one subsample, 37 men were inadvertently given the women's form. All but six items are identical for the women's and men's forms, so that error affected only those six items. For those items, the responses of those 37 men were deleted from further analysis. At the same time, 142 responses from another group of men (Vaillant & McCullough, 1987) were added; for the latter group, the TPRs were retained, rather than recomputed from item distributions. (All had been rated by members of our group.) The Vaillant study used an older form of the test, so the protocols could not be folded into our main sample. They were, however, used in some other items common to the two forms. Because this sample included Harvard graduates, tested in midlife, it added some high-level responses rare in the general population.

Thus, as the experiencd rater becomes familiar with the manual as a whole, including all item manuals, the data from the Vaillant sample appreciably broadens the population range from which examples have been chosen. Accordingly, the conception of ego development is broadened and enriched.

TABLE 3.1

Basic Sample for Manual Revision

Investigator	Number		Age/Grade	Characteristic
	Female	Male		
Beaton	383	97*		Mostly undergraduates at major public urban university
Billington	5		Begun at 37–48	Students in doctoral (counseling?) programs
Chandler	15	19	/College graduates	Technical school graduates, retested after 10 years
Chandler	15	19	/College graduates	College graduates, retested after 10 years
Cohn	15	21	/11& college freshman	Students, lower middle SES
D'Andrea	14	15	10–17/	Inner-city Blacks
Israelievitch	49			Mothers: unmarried welfare, upper middle class & professional
Luchene (Gans)	22	26	college undergraduates	psychology majors
Rogers	64		15–16/10	private girls' school
Rogers	23	14	/10	Private coed school
Novy	175	91	Adults, wide range	Evening students (older), county employees, senior adults, health professionals, adult delinquents, & volunteers
Patterson	21	18		Grad students
Ver Merris	17	28	24–48/	Conservative midwestern theological college, various majors, middle to upper middle SES
Total	818	251		

*Only 51 male subjects for Items 22, 27, 29, 30, 33, 36

THE BASIC PROCESS

The basis for manual construction is the "decoding sheet," the same process used to construct the 1970 manual (see chapter 1). The decoding sheet is a list of all 1,160 responses to a single item, rearranged according to the scoring manual being used. The scoring manual is reproduced with all sample responses to that item listed under the category, where they belong. Within each category the responses are listed in order of the TPR of the protocol on which they appeared. An important difference from the way that the original manual was created is that the revision data included, in addition to data on the new sample, information on how the manual was being used by people in the interested research community, outside our own group.

With this as a starting point, most responses that the previous raters had called unclassifiable were sorted into categories, either ones already there or new categories. Misclassified responses were reclassified correctly to the best of our ability. Complete omissions were rated E4 (Conformist) by default, as before. However, many responses that other researchers considered unratable, we rated. A memorable example was, "The worst thing about being a woman is— she is the default parent." This was called unratable, hence rated E-4; to the computer literate it is a witty answer, probably best rated E-6, or at least E-5. (Even if the rater did not understand that usage of "default," a rating could have been guessed.)

In many cases, a compound response had been rated according to its popular or common part, neglecting the unique element that raised its rating; that is particularly likely to happen with an inexperienced rater. Naturally, a rater feels more secure rating the part of the response that can be found verbatim in the manual, rather than dealing with a complex idea not present verbatim. That is an inevitable hazard of the rating process.

The only cures are long familiarity with the material, including total protocols, and going back over one's item ratings after rating the corresponding total protocol. Rating with a partner, and checking disagreements, with mutual criticism, can also be helpful.

Some old categories showed up as not being used or not used correctly. Most E-8 categories, for example, were used incorrectly. That is not surprising, because answers at that level are almost always unique, and the common elements are not easy to capture in category titles. Fewer E-8 categories are given in the present manual.

Some investigators overestimated the ego level of their subjects; that is one of the hazards of studying groups with whom one has a special or personal relationship.

Many category titles were rewritten. Exemplar titles had been followed more successfully than descriptive titles; so, where possible, descriptive titles were replaced by exemplar ones.

In many cases where a category continued to subsume a significant number of responses, the example used as the title was no longer a good representative of how those ideas are expressed today. In such cases, a currently more typical example was chosen as title.

Some whole categories were moved up or down one level, rarely more, on the basis of the distribution of TPRs in that category. (The distribution of TPRs was, of course, interpreted in terms of the base rates for the sample. See Appendix E.)

Some categories were split. That occurred when it was possible to differentiate in some way the responses that came mostly from protocols with higher TPRs from those that came mostly from protocols with lower TPRs. Most often a simple version of the idea defining the category was at the lower level, a more amplified or qualified version at the higher level.

COMPARISON WITH 1970 MANUAL

Format

The most obvious difference between the current revision and the 1970 manual is the use of themes. They are used to guide raters to the relevant part of the manual, in place of needing to scan all the categories at the appropriate level. They also facilitate comparison across levels for a given topic. Most people who have used both the original manual and the present revision consider themes helpful. However, themes are never completely successful. Responses are too variable to fit neatly into mutually exclusive themes; probably every item has a few responses that best fit some category but not the theme under which the category is listed; in such cases the category governs. Also, themes are idiosyncratic; another person might sort categories differently into similar themes, or might choose altogether different themes.

A second difference is that the present manual is somewhat condensed. It is intended to be more efficient for the rater. The use of many obvious and somewhat redundant examples in the 1970 manual served a pedagogical purpose, convincing readers of the reality of the distinctions being drawn. However, the concept of *ego development* used here has now been expounded in many books and articles and is in less need of defense. The temper of the times has changed, so the chief obstacle to use of the manual is not that people are skeptical of the concept but that the process of scoring cannot be done by computer. Because many wonders can now be accomplished by a couple of keystrokes, mastering a scoring manual conceptually appears to be an unreasonable requirement. (An offer to computerize the scoring manual, given enough data, has been made already, and undoubtedly others will think of the same thing.)

An attempt to computerize scoring was made by an exceptionally knowledgeable user (R. R. Holt). It appeared at first to be successful. However, as soon as the program was applied to a new set of data, it became apparent that the computerized manual worked only for the sample that generated it (R. R. Holt, personal communication, 1990). Thus prime consideration is making the manual efficient and usable.

A similar change is the condensation of the introductory paragraphs to the items, the "blurbs." Blurbs for separate levels of each item are omitted. Most of the omissions reiterated parts of Chapter 2 of volume I (Manifestations of ego level in Sentence Completions) in relation to specific categories of the instant stem. Again, this served a pedagogical purpose but was little help after even short experience.

A fourth difference is that the 1970 manual was closer to the way subjects actually write. All of its data had been gathered by our own group and were carefully transcribed to reproduce as closely as possible exactly what had been written, including all errors of spelling, punctuation, and grammar. As the sources for the present manual included data that had been gathered and transcribed by many investigators, no such guarantee could be given of absolute faithfulness to the original. There was internal evidence that many errors had been introduced by typists. Therefore most major errors have been corrected, except for such widespread usages as "alright" or errors that appeared *prima facie* to be those of the subject. (Overall, spelling, punctuation, and grammar appear to be lost arts. It is probably impossible to be strictly faithful to what the subjects have written and still be intelligible to raters using the manual, and convey the intended range of responses included in each category.)

Samples

The subjects who provided the data for this revision were drawn widely from the social spectrum, but we do not claim they represent the different elements in proportion to their numbers in the population of the United States, any more than did the subjects for the 1970 manual. In fact, we insist that the responses contained in the manual do not constitute a normative sample in any sense.

The largest single source of subjects for most of the subsamples in our present manual construction sample has been students, mostly of college age or older, or college graduates. By way of comparison, many of the subjects in the sample used to derive the 1970 manual were from mothers' groups; half of the women were without college educations. In part that represents different recruitment strategies, but in part that represents a difference in educational level today and differences in what women do. Many more women work during the day and can be found at school or at work rather than in mothers' meetings. School is an easier place to find subjects for a study like this than is the workplace.

Any reservations one might have about the manual's representativeness are mitigated, however, because most categories for most items drew responses from different subsamples, and most drew from both men and women. Thus, internal evidence suggests that the manual is not heavily dependent on the source of subjects.

At the same time, one cannot extrapolate very far to ego levels that are underrepresented. There are fewer E-2, E-3, and E-8 subjects than would be optimal to give a fair representation of the possible answers and modes of thought at those levels.

Therefore, the rater must draw on examples from all items and from theory for guidance for extreme ratings.

Chapter 4

Testing and Revising the Rules for Obtaining TPRs for 36-Item and 18-Item Forms

Lê Xuân Hy
U.S. Government Accounting Office
Kathryn Bobbitt
Private Practice, Waverly, WV
Jane Loevinger
Washington University

In order to test the rules for arriving at total protocol ratings (TPRs), Hy and Bobbitt (1991) assembled a group of 13 subsamples that had been tested using the old SCT Form (Form 11-68). The pooled sample for Study 1 comprised 502 male and 526 female participants, ranging from school-aged to middle-aged, with many college students, and with other subjects drawn from varied sources. For the pooled sample, E-levels ranged from E-2 ($n = 18$) to E-9 ($n = 14$), with most cases at E-5 and E-6, as is usually the case for college students. All of the protocols had been assigned a final TPR by consensus of experienced raters. Those final TPRs constituted the criterion for testing the rules for going from item ratings to TPRs.

Originally, in the 1970 manual, in addition to the standard ogive rules, there were borderline rules, that is, a table indicating borderline cases where raters were encouraged to use other clues from the protocol to overrule the automatic ogive TPR, if they intuitively deemed the particular protocol convincingly different from those for which the automatic ogive TPR was appropriate.

The Hy–Bobbitt study showed that using the borderline rules led to more rather than fewer errors in TPR, as judged by agreement with the previously agreed consensus final TPRs. Therefore, in the current manual revision, borderline rules

TABLE 4.1

Automatic Ogive and ISS Rules to Assign TPR for 36-Item and 18-Item Forms

Level	Item Sum	Automatic Ogive[a]	Explanations of Ogive[a,b]
		For 36-Item Forms[c]	
E9 Integrated	235 & up	No more than 34 ratings at E8[d]	2 or more E9[d]
E8 Autonomous	217–234	No more than 31 ratings at E7	5 or more E8 or higher
E7 Individualistic	201–216	No more than 30 ratings at E6	6 or more E7 or higher
E6 Conscientious	181–200	No more than 24 ratings at E5	12 or more E6 or higher
E5 Self-Aware	163–180	No more than 20 ratings at E4	16 or more E5 or higher
E2 Impulsive	72–132	At least 5 ratings at E2	5 or more E2
E3 Self-Protective	133–145	At least 6 ratings at E3	6 or more E3 or lower
E4 Conformist	146–162	Other cases	Other cases
		For 18-Item Forms	
E9 Integrated	119 & up	No more than 17 ratings at E8[d,e]	1 or more E9[d,e]
E8 Autonomous	109–118	No more than 16 ratings at E7	2 or more E8 or higher
E7 Individualistic	101–108	No more than 15 ratings at E6	3 or more E7 or higher
E6 Conscientious	91–100	No more than 12 ratings at E5	6 or more E6 or higher
E5 Self-Aware	82–90	No more than 9 ratings at E4	9 or more E5 or higher
E2 Impulsive	36–67	At least 3 ratings at E2	3 or more E2
E3 Self-Protective	68–75	At least 3 ratings at E3	3 or more E3 or lower
E4 Conformist	76–81	Other cases	Other cases

Note.
[a]Apply ogive rule in the order given, from E9 to E4.
[b]The explanations for ogive should yield identical results to the automatic ogive.
[c]Automatic ogive for 36-item forms appeared in Loevinger and Wessler (1970, p. 129).
[d]To receive an E9 rating by ogive rule, the E8 ogive criterion must also be met.
[e]TPR based on a single and extreme item rating is unreliable.

have been dropped. The data from (Hy–Bobbitt) Study 1 were also used to set parameters for translating Item Sum Scores (ISS) into TPRs (Table 4.1)

Data from this (Hy–Bobbitt) study plus other considerations led to dropping between-stage ratings, such as I-3/4 and Delta-3, which had been presumed to indicate transitions between stages, although often resorted to simply as compromise ratings. There never had been any evidence that such "transitional" ratings were in fact less stable than others. The Hy–Bobbitt data suggested, to the contrary, that those between stage ratings are as stable as any others.

In addition to ogive rules and item-sums, other possible scoring algorithms were also examined; Hy and Bobbitt concluded that the automatic ogive rules were the best, that is, most likely to match the consensus ratings by expert, experienced raters.

SCORING SHORT FORM SCTs

As there had never been an adequate basis for assigning TPRs to short form tests, which are used by many investigators, Hy and Bobbitt arbitrarily treated each page of the Form 11-68 protocols in their study as if it were an 18-item test. They then made ogive rules for 18-item tests and set TPR parameters for ISSs for 18-item tests, optimizing agreement between TPRs thus obtained and the criterion scores, which fortunately were available for all these protocols.

A second study used 10 subsamples collected and scored by investigators in different parts of the country, all using the new Form 81.

The pooled sample for Study 2 comprised 686 participants (about equally divided between males and females) ranging in E-level from E-2 ($n = 19$), to E-9 ($n = 2$).

The item ratings were assumed to be correct, but new TPRs were calculated, using a macro to obtain an automatic ogive TPR. These macro-generated ogive TPRs were used as criterion, a decision justified by their first study.

Unlike previous forms of the SCT, Form 81 had been designed for the two pages to be used as separate 18-item forms.

Study 2 was used to cross-validate the ogive rules and item-sum parameters derived from Study 1. The ogive rules and item sum parameters presented in this manual (Table 4.1) were derived from these studies.

The conclusions were as follows:

1. For 36-item forms, ogive TPRs are superior to item-sum TPRs, and to all other scoring algorithms.
2. For 18-item forms, item-sum TPRs are superior to the ogive rules.
3. The total 36-item form yields more accurate TPRs than any 18-item form can, a result foretold by elementary reliability theory.

Forms with fewer than 18 items can safely be assumed to be even less good.

Chapter 5
Reliability and Validity of the SCT

Jane Loevinger
Washington University

The method of scoring and interpreting the SCT presented in this manual is essentially the same as that in the original 1970 SCT manual (Loevinger & Wessler, 1970). Detailed data on the homogeneity, reliability, and validity of the SCT were presented there and in subsequent reviews, principally those of Hauser (1976) and Loevinger (1979). The main points of those reviews are summarized, but it is unnecessary to repeat the full details of those reports.

Major evidence for the construct validity of the SCT was reviewed under the headings of substantive validity, structural validity, and external validity. This chapter also includes the additional approach of clinical validity, and new evidence concerning the current version of the SCT, Form 81.

SUBSTANTIVE VALIDITY

Substantive validity is essentially what used to be called *content validity,* except that instead of being an alternative kind of validity, it is construed as a component of construct validity.

Probably the intuitive appeal of the construct of ego development, as it has been presented in various places, is what has drawn many psychologists and other researchers to use or investigate the use of the SCT for its measurement. That kind of intuitive appeal is probably a necessary ingredient of substantive validity, but it is not sufficient to establish the SCT's validity.

The test consists not only of the set of sentence stems, many of which are not unique to this test, but also the task set to the subject, the instructions to the subject, and the scoring instructions, such as are given in the original or the present scoring manual.

The sentence stems were in some cases borrowed from other sentence completion tests, and they were supplemented by other stems appropriate to the studies of young women with which the project began. However, there has been no indication that the validity of the test hinges in any way on choice of particular stems; on the contrary, all efforts to set apart the function of some stems as distinct from others have failed.

The use of a projective rather than an objective test is justified by the fact that, in this context, ego development is taken to mean (or perhaps to reflect) the person's frame of reference; thus a format requiring the subject to project his or her own frame of reference is preferable to providing a clearly stated set of questions, reflecting the test constructor's frame of reference.

The conception is closer to an Adlerian conception of the ego than a Freudian one, and it is also close to H. Sullivan's (1953) conception of the *Self-System*. In fact, the scale of "interpersonal integration" (C. Sullivan et al., 1957), which provided our starting point, was explicitly derived from the study of H. Sullivan's (1953) *Interpersonal Theory of Psychiatry,* as its name suggests.

Evidence for the coherence and thus substantive validity includes the following:

1. New raters can be trained to be almost the equal of trained raters, using only written instructions and prescribed practice exercises. That is possible because the conception is coherent enough to be communicable.
2. Trained, very experienced raters can do about as well with items for which there is no manual as they do with manual items, even though they have only the conception of ego development as guide, plus what they remember of how similar responses to other stems have been scored.

That does not work for people using only stage names as guide. The conception is embodied in the scoring manual, and it is absorbed by practice in scoring, not by reading vague, abstract descriptions of the concept, much less by just using stage names.

Each stage represents a complex structure of several strands, including impulse control, interpersonal relations, and conscious preoccupations. Some conformity may be found at every stage, and we certainly do not mean to imply that people of the Conformist stage do not have any conscience, in the usual sense of that word.

In order to avoid neologisms as stage names, we have named stages after common human functions that are prominent at the given stage, but they are such common functions that they must be present at other stages, perhaps to some degree at all stages.

The chief problem with our practice in that respect is that an occasional user is led to believe that stage names suffice to classify without a scoring manual. The results are disastrously wrong.

Similarly, at the time, early on, that there was only a manual made for women, using exclusively female samples, trained raters could score male samples just as well, as judged by their agreement with other trained raters and with final total protocol ratings (TPRs).

The major evidence for the *structural component* of validity is homogeneity (i.e., internal consistency). For the sealed sample, used in the original validational study of the SCT, the alpha coefficient for the 36-item test was .91.

A principal component analysis showed one major component, with an eigen value of 8.8, accounting for more than 20% of the total variance. The second principal component had an eigen value of only 1.2, compatible with being a chance deviation from zero. Scaled scores on the first principal component are essentially the same as the sum of item ratings ($r = .999$).

The unity of the test is created by the method, that is, internal consistency was the criterion used repeatedly in refining the manual, so that all the items necessarily tend to reflect the same underlying variable, that represented by the TPR.

Despite the unity of the test, assured by the method, some researchers have sought subsets of items to measure different postulated aspects of ego development. Lambert (1972), using Kohlberg's (1964) test of moral maturity and the SCT with Kohlberg's longitudinal sample, which is a large and diverse sample, sought a "moral" subset of items. The SCT items correlated about as well with the Kohlberg score as with the TPR on the SCT; so Lambert concluded that there is no subset of "moral" items.

Blasi (1971) separated the SCT items a priori into a set of 13 or 14 that seemed to reflect "responsibility" and all the others. He computed Item Sum Scores (ISS) separately for the two subsets of items, for the subjects in his study. He found the item subsets were not statistically distinct; so he concluded there was no subset of "responsibility" items.

One structural issue unique to developmental variables is sequentiality. Evidence for sequentiality comprises (a) cross-sectional age differences, the minimal and most obvious evidence, but not crucial; (b) retests in longitudinal studies; (c) change following theory-relevant interventions; and (d) asymmetry of comprehension.

Cross-Sectional Age Differences.   Studies showing cross-sectional increase by grade and thus presumably also age have been done with school children in Toronto, Canada, both boys and girls, ages 10 to 18 years; and with Black inner-city youths, male and female, Grades 7, 8, 9, 10; and with students at a boys' prep school, Grades 8, 9, and 11.

Retests in Longitudinal Studies.   Several high school samples retested after intervals of between 1½ and 6 years, showed a significant gain, approximately proportional to the time between initial test and retest. Most also showed a significant correlation between test and retest (Redmore & Loevinger, 1979).

At the college level, several classes at a technical institute were tested as entering freshmen; most classes showed a significant gain when retested after 2 years of college, but no further rise after Year 4 (Loevinger, 1978).

Theory-Relevant Interventions.   The most interesting studies of sequentiality are those that involve theory-relevant interventions between test and retest.

Blasi (1971, 1976), pretested sixth-grade Black inner-city children and created several groups of between five and eight children at the Impulsive (E-2), Self-Protective (E-3), and Conformist (E-4) levels, and a single group at the Self-Aware (E-5) level. Blasi devised stage-appropriate moral dilemmas, and had the children in each group enact the appropriate ones, and then followed the role-playing with inquiry and discussion. Two observers recorded independently what went on in each group. Each group met for 10 sessions over a 2-week period. Although a retest after the 2-week experiment did not demonstrate a significant rise in ego level for the group as a whole, the observations recorded during the experiment provide a rich source of behavioral manifestations of the various levels.

The Impulsive (E-2) groups lacked insight into motives, had short attention spans, were restless, disrupted the sessions and giggled thoughtlessly. They had no difficulty seeing themselves as causes of negative behaviors, but they shifted the blame. They were most interested in attacking each other and in a chance to "rat" on each other to the experimenter. In playing the role of authority, they recommended very harsh punishments.

The Self-Protective (E-3) children were good at role-playing, especially the role of the sneaky or opportunistic hero. They were concerned with being found out and protecting themselves. When they were caught, they demanded indulgence and leniency, but as authorities they were harshly punitive. They could not portray shame but were instead sullen or defiant. When they were supposed to be authorities arousing shame, they just screamed, even though they saw it just caused anger.

The Conformist (E-4) children were more interested in the rules than were children of lower levels, but they could only see literal interpretations, limited to obedience. In addition to avoiding punishment, they saw love for and loyalty to authority as a reason for obedience. They were not angry or hostile to authority, but they were scornful of liberal interpretation of rules, which they considered two-faced or indecisive.

The small group of children at the Self-Aware (E-5) level, were more similar to the Conformists than to the others, but they were more disapproving of sneaky and pragmatic attitudes.

A number of studies by Mosher and Sprinthal (1971) involve what they called *deliberate psychological education.* These are courses that include some lectures and a practicum, such as peer counseling or teaching children of lower grades. There is also an attempt to give the students insight into their own problems. The students were pretested and posttested with Kohlberg's test and the SCT. There were gains in both, as compared to control classes that did not register gains in either test in the same period of time.

Lasker (1977) and his associates created an organizational development program based on ego development theory, which they used in some companies on the island of Curaçao. They found the modal pretest for Curaçaon workers was between Self-Protective (E-3) and Conformist (E-4) stages, and the modal level for staff members was at the Self-Aware (E-5) level. Their training program, lasting several months, achieved a small rise in ego level for those who began below the Conformist stage, but no evidence for any rise above the Conformist stage. It is understandable that a training program built around group meetings would facilitate a rise to the Conformist level, but not to any Postconformist level.

Asymmetry of Comprehension. A final line of evidence for sequentiality is asymmetry of comprehension, that is, people can understand thinking at their own level or at levels below their own, but not at levels above their own. Blasi's subjects found it difficult to play roles higher than their own level, and sometimes would distort the story to eliminate such characters, or misunderstand the story or the role.

Redmore (1976) gave the SCT under normal conditions to several small groups, and then retested them asking them either to make a good impression or a bad impression. When asked to make a bad impression, most of these fairly sophisticated subjects lowered their scores somewhat, often to the Self-Protective level. When asked to make a good impression, their scores either stayed the same or made a very small rise of about half a stage. A few women, particularly those originally above the Conformist level, lowered their scores under instructions to make a good impression. The fact that it is easier for people to lower their scores than raise them is evidence for asymmetry of comprehension.

EXTERNAL VALIDITY

The external variables with which the SCT has been correlated include, among others, (a) interview estimates of ego level, (b) objective tests, (c) projective tests, (d) tests of other developmental-stage theories, and (e) behavioral measures.

Interviews. Several investigators who are knowledgeable and experienced with the SCT scoring manual have made global judgment of ego level of persons they have interviewed without knowledge of their SCT responses or scores. In some cases there was also another rater for the interview, who worked from a transcript, also without knowledge of the subjects' SCTs. The samples were as varied as college freshmen women in a psychology class, men in an engineering school, and 16-year-old girls in a parochial high school. Correlations with the SCT varied from .32 to .51. Considering that there has been no scoring manual for judging ego level from interviews, those correlations are as high as could be expected.

Rock (1975) performed an interesting variation on interviews as validation for the SCT with 50 undergraduate women, selected so as to maximize variability in ego level. Each woman was recorded while talking about a neutral topic; when the tape was played back to her, she was asked what her voice and manner of speech told about her. Her responses were taped again, and scored on an ad hoc scale of "self-confrontation." She was then asked to tell stories to six TAT cards, according to standard instructions. Then the theory of projection was explained to her, and her stories were read back to her, one at a time. She was asked to interpret each story in terms of her experiences. Responses were scored by an adaptation of the TAT self-interpretation score of Luborsky (1953). She was then given Heath's (1968) Perceived Self Questionnaire, which is another measure of personal maturity, and she was also given, as a measure of intelligence, a subtest from the WAIS. The two measures of self-insight correlated almost as highly with the SCT (.53 and .52) as they did with each other. The correlations remained highly significant when intelligence or age was partialled out. Heath's test correlated .44 with the SCT.

Rock concluded that subjects at the Conformist or Preconformist levels tended to be unreflective about their experience or reflective in nonpsychological terms. Some of those at the Self-Aware stage reflected on themselves in more psychological terms, as did most of those at the Conscientious stage, and almost all of those at higher levels, who often had a dynamic understanding of themselves.

Lasker (1978), who began by working with McClelland's motivation training groups, using the TAT, had noted that the standard categories into which achievement themes were classed formed a hierarchical series. It was this finding that led him to explore the SCT for ego development. He found that the need for achievement scores were low for people below the Conformist stage and rose sharply up to the Conscientious stage, where they peaked. The power motive, in contrast, peaked at the transition from Self-Protective to Conformist stage. The affiliation motive differed from both of the above.

Kohlberg's (1969) Moral Judgment Instrument is by far the best known of other developmental stage tests. It has been correlated with the SCT in more than one study. Lambert, in order to tap the full range of Kohlberg's test and the SCT, used six subsamples differing widely in age and education. The correlation between the two tests over the whole range was .80. The correlation in a subsample of 11- and 15-year-olds was .46. That suggested that the correlation between the two tests varied with age. His data for the whole range, with age partialled out, yielded a correlation of .60.

In a younger sample, E. Sullivan, McCullough, and Stager (1970) found a correlation of the SCT with Kohlberg's test of .40 with age partialled out. In the same study, they also used Hunt's conceptual level questionnaire, which correlated .23 with the SCT when age was partialled out.

Behavioral Measures If a test predicts nothing except other tests, it has limited validity. There have been some nontest behaviors associated with the SCT in several of the studies just reviewed. Conformity and delinquency are behaviors with expected relations to the SCT.

Frank and Quinlan (1976) compared delinquent adolescent girls with girls in two control groups matched for age, social class, and ethnic background. They were given the SCT orally. The raters did not know which girls were the delinquents. Many girls in all three groups were at the Self-Protective level, but at the Impulsive level there were 12 delinquent girls, but only one from each of their control groups. The overall number of deviant behaviors correlated -.45 with ego stage; fighting, by itself, correlated -.52.

Powitzky (1975) studied young male offenders in federal custody. He hypothesized that ego level would increase in line with the offense, from car thieves and bank robbers through drug offenders, to embezzlers, and conscientious objectors. His hypothesis was confirmed, although he was surprised that embezzlers were so close in ego level to conscientious objectors, who served as the normal control here. None of the conscientious objectors scored below the Conformist Stage but 21 of the 92 other offenders did.

Mikel (1974) tested 107 inmates of a county prison outside a major midwestern city. Staff members, but not guards, filled out adjective checklist descriptions of men they knew well. Descriptions of the behavior of the men at various levels can be drawn in terms of adjectives used relatively more often for men who tested at the given level.

Preconformists as a group were described as rebellious, unrealistic, immature, and untrustworthy. Those at the Impulsive stage were described as easily provoked, undisciplined, and impulsive. Those at the Self-Protective stage were more likely to be seen as gregarious and critical of procedures. Those at the Conformist and Self-Aware levels were seen as adjusted, not rebellious, and dogmatic. The 14 men (13%) at the Postconformist levels, were seen as truthful and receptive to counseling.

CLINICAL VALIDATION

Hauser, Powers, and Noam (1991) presented a remarkably extensive clinical validational study. They studied a varied group of adolescents over several years, including SCTs for the youths and their parents and recordings of family interactions in an experimental situation, where the family was asked to agree on a common solution to a hypothetical dilemma. The correspondence between the actual family interactions and what could have been anticipated from their SCTs is remarkable.

The cases were chosen to represent a range of developmental levels and developmental trajectories, including some subjects who gained in ego level over the period studied, some who lost, and some who held steady. Thus, their study is an unusually extensive and impressive clinical validation, although its value is not readily expressed in a single coefficient.

STUDIES USING FORM 81

Novy and Francis (1992) explored the psychometric properties of the SCT Form 81. In a sample of 265 adults drawn from a wide social spectrum, including college students and faculty, adult delinquents, and health professionals. Ego levels covered a wide range, from six people at the Impulsive level (E-2), to three at the Autonomous level (E-8).

In addition to the SCT, the participants responded to eight objective tests (format either agree–disagree or degree of agreement), each test putatively measuring an aspect of personality presumed to be an aspect of ego development as measured by the SCT, such as impulsivity, interpersonal sensitivity, toleration for ambiguity, or interest in diverse thinking.

The first half of the SCT had an item sum mean of 104.3, the second half, 104.7, with variances of 138.8 and 127.5, respectively. Coefficient alpha was .84, .81, and .90 for the first half, second half, and total of 36 items, respectively. Interrater agreement on the 36-item sum was .94. The correlation between the two halves was .79, which rose to .96 when disattenuated for unreliability.

The eight objective tests were correlated with each half of the SCT separately and with the 36-item total. Corresponding correlations were so similar as to suggest the equivalence of the halves to each other and their virtual equivalence to the 36-item total.

Novy concluded that the two half tests are usable as equivalent forms and that each is usable as a measure of ego development comparable to the 36-item form, despite loss of reliability due to shorter length.

In a further study of 229 subjects, using 12 objective tests (data partly overlapping the previous study), Novy (1993) performed a principal component analysis on the objective tests. The first principal component had an eigen value of 3.41, accounting for 28% of the variance. The SCT Form 81 was scored by the ogive rules, with an interrater agreement of .94. Correlation between scores on the first principal component of the objective tests and the SCT TPRs was .35, significant at the .001 level.

Using other data from the same broad sample as the above studies, Novy (1992) performed analyses comparable to those in Loevinger (1985), and concluded that the men's Form 81 and the women's Form 81 are comparable, not biased with respect to gender. Whatever initial bias in favor of women may have resulted from the fact that those who constructed the test and its scoring manual and did the first work on the test were all women, as were all their original subjects, has now been compensated by recent revisions, which was the major aim in constructing Form 81.

In a study of the robustness of the SCT under manipulation of instructions, Blumentritt, Novy, Gaa, and Liberman (1996) readministered the SCT to groups of students about 1 week after their original testing. In the control group, for whom the test was readministered with the standard instructions to just complete the sentences, the retest r was .72 for the ISS and .79 for the ogive TPR. By either measure, there was a slight nonsignificant decrement on retest.

One experimental group was told to complete the sentences as an integrated person would; they were given a one-page description of an integrated person, drawn from Maslow's (1954) description of a self-actualizing person. The other experimental group was told to complete the sentences in the most complex and thought-provoking way they could. The majority of those in the experimental groups either showed no change in TPR or increased by about one level. The two experimental groups differed significantly from the control group but not from each other.

To put those findings in context, note that the SCT comprises not only the sentence stems but also the instructions and the scoring method. Therefore, changing the instructions, as was done in the two experimental groups, changes the test. The material in the present scoring manual is intended for the original test, with the original instructions. An interpretation of a given TPR implies that the test was given with the original instructions, to just complete the sentences. Any psychological test can be spoiled by coaching. In effect the altered instructions given to the experimental groups were an example of coaching.

Weiss, Zilberg, and Genevro (1989) have used the SCT Form 81 along with other tests in studying an adult outpatient sample drawn from clinics and private practices in the San Francisco Bay area. Subjects were paid to participate, but they were also offered, and most chose, to have their therapists informed of their assessments.

The subjects varied widely in age; the mean age of the 20 men was 38.5 years, and of the 22 women, 36.8 years. The mean educational attainment for both men and women was some college. The SCT was the first test given; the complete 36-item form was given, and standard instructions were used.

Subjects were given a retest of the SCT some time between a week and a couple of months after the original test. Instructions for the retest were to "be as candid" as they were the first time, but to disregard their first answers. Two raters rated each protocol, and a third rater helped to resolve any disagreements. The range of TPRs was wide, from Impulsive to Integrated(E-9), but most were at the Self-Aware or Conscientious level. Interrater reliability was similar to what has been attained in studies with nonpsychiatric samples, as was test–retest reliability, and also internal consistency (alpha coefficient).

OBSTACLES TO AND PROBLEMS OF VALIDITY

Outside variables that correlate with a test score may be distortions of the measurement, in which case, the lower the correlation, the more valid the test, or they may be an intrinsic part of what the test measures, in which case the test cannot be valid if the correlation is low. The problem is to distinguish between those cases.

As a concrete example, many researchers have noted a correlation between some measure of intelligence and the SCT. What does that import? Is intelligence necessary to reach higher levels of ego development? Or, less plausibly, does high ego development permit attainment of higher intelligence scores? Although that is implausible, it is not at all impossible that persons at the lowest ego levels would have trouble staying in school after reaching the minimum required by law. One cannot expect to find many Impulsive level students in college.

The other extraneous variable that is most often pointed to is *verbal fluency*, that is, many users discover that there is a high correlation between the length of the sentence completions and the scored ego level of the response. The correlation between number of words and ego level does not prove that one could do just as well counting words as using the scoring manual. The answers that display high ego level are complex thoughts about relationships, about development, about psychological causation, and the like. Simple remarks about "fun" or "happy " or "sad " or "mad," and the like can be expressed in a brief phrase, as they often are on protocols of Preconformist subjects. The number of words is not extraneous to the display of high ego level in such cases.

For the sealed sample, Loevinger and Wessler (1970) found the sum of item word counts was more reliable ($\alpha = .95$) than the sum of item ratings ($\alpha = .91$). However, the correlation with criterion TPR for the word count sum was (.58), whereas for the sum of item ratings, the correlation with criterion TPR was .93. Thus, scoring items by the manual produces a better approximation to the criterion TPR than counting words. The combination of high reliability but lower validity is evidence that word count operates as a distortion of measurement.

A more difficult case is socioeconomic status. Higher SCT scores have been found for subjects in higher social and economic strata in studies done in Japan, in Curaçao, and in the United States. At present, no conclusion is warranted, except that the finding is repeated in many places, but what that implies is not certain.

MOTIVATION AND CONDITIONS OF TESTING

Redmore and Waldman (1975) did several small studies of short-term retest effects. When the retest occurred 1 to 2 weeks after the original test, there was a tendency for scores to decline about half a stage, particularly for scores above the Conformist level. The researchers reasoned that the elaborations and qualifications that characterize responses above the Conformist level are just what a person bored with being asked to repeat the test would be apt to omit. The one group that showed no decline was a psychology class to which the retest was introduced as a study of test reliability.

In a study of students in an engineering college, the SCT was given to students during the registration process on one occasion. The situation proved too chaotic for optimal cooperation, and that mistake was not repeated. Many of the test protocols, when analyzed later, showed an excess of low level responses, often ones expressing hostility to the test or tester. Comparison of these protocols with those of similar classes from the same college, tested under more favorable circumstances, confirmed that the group tested during registration had an excess of preconformist ratings.

Weiss et al. (1989) provided another circumstance relevant to achieving optimal motivation for cooperation. Their subjects were assured that their assessments would be made available to their therapists, if the patient so chose.

The foregoing considerations concern ways to ensure that the test subjects will respond to the test in a way that provides the optimal measure of their basic ego level.

The hazard of retesting in too short a time and without a satisfactory explanation is that the TPR will show a spurious decline in circumstances where a real decline in ego level is extremely improbable. That is an example of one of the difficulties in carrying out longitudinal research in this area. Obviously, longitudinal studies are important in validating any developmental sequence, as reviewers often urge.

As was remarked earlier, the SCT is vulnerable to distortion in another direction too. When the retest is given with elaborate instructions to the subject to give his or her best and most complex or elaborate ideas, or the like, the person has virtually been coached in how to achieve high ego level scores.

Because most work has been done with the standard instructions, it seems reasonable to assume that such validity as the SCT has demonstrated is best achieved by adhering to standard instructions.

The hazard in altering instructions as a way to raise ego levels is that it is too easy for researchers who set out to prove that their favorite programs for improving other people's character has in fact raised ego levels. All such claims must be carefully monitored for the integrity of the testing process.

Chapter 6
Managing SCT Data

◆ ◆ ◆

Lê Xuân Hy
U.S. Government Accounting Office

This chapter describes the way to process the SCT data in an easy and accurate manner. It also provides a few tips on how to use a computer spreadsheet to accomplish the task. The overall process of rating a protocol is clear: rating each item first (chapter 4 and Appendix A in Hy & Loevinger, 1996), then deriving total protocol ratings (TPRs; chapter 5 and Appendix B, Hy & Loevinger, 1996). There are, however, other steps to prepare for both the item rating and the TPR.

THE PROCESS OF MANAGING SCT DATA

The steps required in managing SCT data are discussed here.

Check the Completions. If there are six or more omissions, the protocol should not be used. The test administrator may want to check the number of omissions before accepting a protocol, and encourage those who have slightly more than five omissions to provide a few more completions. The administrator may also want to check legibility.

Type Up Item Response Lists (IRLs). Responses should be typed verbatim, including misspelled words. Appendix A in Hy and Loevinger (1996) gives examples of IRLs. The primary purpose of IRLs is to separate each response from the complete protocol in order to rate the response independently. In order to enhance this independence, the order of the responses should be varied from IRL to IRL, so that, for example, the first response on each IRL does not come from the same protocol. If the order is not varied, raters may notice a certain pattern (high or low responses, or a particular writing style) somewhere in the IRLs, especially near the beginning or the end. Similarly, the identifications (IDs) should be omitted or printed in such a way that raters can easily ignore them to arrive at independent item ratings.

Omit Data. Certain data should be omitted during typing to enhance other types of independence. For example, if you are testing whether race has an influence on ego development, the response "I am—a student from China" should be typed as "a student from [location]." Another example is age. Raters should rate responses without taking age into account. Thus, the response "I am–13 years old" should be typed as "[number] years old." Although the omission of age is not important for that stem because the manual clearly rates that response at E4m, it may influence the impressionistic rating of the total protocol, which will be described later. Some other data, such as proper names, should also be omitted to protect confidentiality.

Insert Notes and Comments. If the typists cannot decipher the handwriting at all, or are not sure if it is one word or another, they should insert a note. In the case of a translated response, sometimes several translations are equally likely; that should also be noted.

Interrater Reliability. There should be two independent raters, each of whom records both the E-level and the category for each rating, such as 4m. The two ratings are compared. If they agree on the E-level, the categories are kept for other purposes (such as validation of the manual) but only the E-level is used toward the calculation of the TPR and interrater reliability. If they disagree on the E-level, then they should discuss and arrive at an agreed level rating. Having recorded the categories of their original ratings should facilitate the discussion.

Several measures of the interrater reliability can be used. One is the correlation between the two ratings. Another familiar index is the percentages of agreement at the same level, within two levels, and within three or more levels. In addition, the mean ratings can also be compared to see whether one rater tends to give higher rating than another.

If for some reason the two raters cannot agree, a third and more experienced rater can decide on the final rating. At times when rating is expected to be unusually difficult, such as novice raters or rating translated responses from an unfamiliar culture, the two raters might want to meet and discuss after rating a small sample of the responses. In that case, however, interrater reliability should be calculated separately for the training sample and for the rest.

Total Protocol Rating. Two sources of information are used in deriving the TPRs: the distribution of item ratings, and the nonpsychometric signs (see chapter 5, p. 39, Item 9, in Hy & Loevinger, 1996). In order to evaluate the nonpsychometric signs, the whole protocol should be typed out together, except for the required omissions described previously.

The steps discussed here can all be done with a typewriter, as was done in the first 20 years of research on this topic. With the help of a personal computer, however, after some practice, the task is faster and easier.

USING COMPUTERS TO MANAGE SCT DATA

Parts of the procedure can be quite intuitive even for novice computer users. For example, the responses can be sorted by item numbers to generate IRLs, and then by ID to generate TPRs. Other parts might be less obvious, such as using a macro to derive automatic TPRs. The following instruction requires only a beginning level of familiarity with computer applications (but a thorough understanding of the process of managing SCT data just presented), and can be used with different spreadsheets and databases. The macro examples, however, are given for Microsoft Excel. This set of macros and their updated version can be viewed and downloaded directly from the World Wide Web at http:// members.aol.com/cmhs 2000 /staff/ hy/ sct macro.html.

Using a Spreadsheet. The easiest computer application to manage SCT in is probably a spreadsheet, such as those in Quatro Pro or Excel. All steps described here can be performed with a spreadsheet alone. Those who are more experienced with integrated packages might want to type the responses into a word processor, such as Word or WordPerfect, because it is slightly easier to type into a word processor than into a spreadsheet. If the data is saved with the proper format (consult with the documentation for importing data for the spreadsheet or database program you are using), the IRL can be directly imported into the proper column in the spreadsheet. Note that if a word processor is used for data entry, the spellchecker should only be used to help identify transcription errors. The final data set should be carefully compared to the original so that the integrity of the data is maintained.

One important limitation of many spreadsheets is that a cell cannot hold more than 254 characters, which is sufficient for almost all normal SCT responses. There are various ways to deal with the exceptional long responses. One way is to use a database, which can have unlimited fields but is more complicated. A simpler way is to use two adjacent cells in two columns to keep each response on one line or "record," thus simplifying various sorting processes in later steps (although printing can be cumbersome). Excel for Office 97 can hold 32,000 characters in each cell.

Most spreadsheets can hold many protocols. For example, Excel 5 can have up to 16,384 rows, or about 450 protocols, per sheet. Excel for Office 97 can have more than 65,000 rows.

Preparing a Spreadsheet. Twelve columns are needed to record gender, ID, item number, item rating for each of two raters (with E-level and category in separate columns), final E-level item rating, the response, response overflow, ogive, and TPR. Macro Prepare sets up these 12 columns, names them, and resizes them (see Fig. 6.1 and Table 6.1).

Se x	ID	Ite m	E1	C1	E2	C2	EF	Response1	Resp onse2	O gi ve	TPR/Su m
	0	1						Item 1. When a child will not join in group activities			
	0	2						Item 2. Raising a family			
	0	3						Item 3. When I am criticized			
	0	4						Item 4. A man's job			
	0	5						Item 5. Being with other people			
	0	6						Item 6. The thing I like about myself is			
	0	7						Item 7. My mother and I			
	0	8						Item 8. What gets me into trouble is			
	0	9						Item 9. Education			
	0	10						Item 10. When people are helpless			
	0	11						Item 11. Women are lucky because			
	0	12						Item 12. A good father			
	0	13						Item 13. A girl has a right to			
	0	14						Item 14. When they talked about sex, I			
	0	15						Item 15. A wife should			
	0	16						Item 16. I feel sorry			
	0	17						Item 17. A man feels good when			
	0	18						Item 18. Rules are			
	0	19						Item 19. Crime and delinquency could be halted if			
	0	20						Item 20. Men are lucky because			
	0	21						Item 21. I just can't stand people who			
	0	22						Item 22. At times she (he) worries about			
	0	23						Item 23. I am			
	0	24						Item 24. A woman feels good when			
	0	25						Item 25. My main problem is			
	0	26						Item 26. A husband has a right to			
	0	27						Item 27. The worst thing about being a woman (man)			
	0	28						Item 28. A good mother			
	0	29						Item 29. When I am with a man (woman)			
	0	30						Item 30. Sometimes she (he) wished that			
	0	31						Item 31. My father			
	0	32						Item 32. If I can't get what I want			
	0	33						Item 33. Usually she (he) feels that sex			
	0	34						Item 34. For a woman a career is			
	0	35						Item 35. My conscience bothers me if			
	0	36						Item 36. A woman (man) should always			
m	1	1									
m	1	2									
m	1	3									
m	1	4									
m	1	5									

FIG. 6.1. The spreadsheet after setting up.

TABLE 6.1
WUSCT Data-Processing Procedures and Corresponding Macros

Step	Macro	Tasks
1	[none]	Check for legibility and number of omissions.
2	Prepare	Type in the following column headings: Gender, ID, Item, E1, C1, E2, C2, EF, Response1, Response2, Ogive, TPR/Sum. Resize column Response1 wide and other columns narrow.
3	Stems	Type in a protocol with ID of 0, Item 1 to 36, and Response1 are 36 stems preceded by two blank spaces and the stem number.
4	[none]	Type in the ID and gender of a protocol once.
5	Protocol	Copy the ID and gender value to the next 35 lines. Type into the item column values 1 to 36.
6	[none]	Type the responses into the Response1 column. Use column Response2 for long responses, if necessary.
7	IRL	Sort the whole worksheet by item, then by Response1.
8	[none]	Rate the responses and type in the E-levels and categories from each rater into separate columns. Identify disagreement between raters and find a final item rating. Calculate interrater reliability and mean rating per rater.
9	SortID	Resort the whole worksheet back by ID, then by item.
10	TPR	Select and copy 36 final item ratings in Column 8 for each protocol. Paste these 36 ratings in Column 11 and sort them in descending order. Derive an ogive TPR and put it in Column 12 on the line of the first response. Sum up the 36 ratings and put this ISS on the next line in Column 12. Derive an item-sum TPR and put it below the ISS in Column 12.

Typing the Stems.   Some people always type the stem in front of each response, such as "I am—a student." That system looks good, especially in a total protocol. However, it has also a number of disadvantages. The first stem, for example, already takes about 50 characters, or about one fifth of the 254-character limit in a cell. An alternative is to list each stem only once at the beginning of each IRL. In order to do that, one can create a protocol with an ID of 0 and with 36 stems in the response column. Preceding each stem are a few blank spaces, so that when sorted by responses the stems would be listed first. Macro Stems creates this ID of 0 with 36 stems as responses.

Typing Gender, ID, and Item Numbers.   Each ID needs to be typed in only once and then copied to the next 35 lines, which is called *filled down* in some spreadsheet programs. After gender and ID of a respondent are typed in and the cursor is in the next blank cell (the item number column), Macro Protocol can be used to copy the gender and ID to the next 35 lines and to add the stem numbers 1 to 36.

Saving a Copy of the Data.   After all data are typed and before any sorting or other manipulation, a copy should be made on a disk of the complete data set. It should be labeled clearly with a date, and set aside in a safe place. Two copies in two places are even better than one. This backup file should not be used for computation or research. It should be reserved solely to recover the original data in case a serious mistake occurs in processing.

Sorting the Responses Into IRLs, After the Responses are Typed In.
Sorting is one of the most powerful tools, and thus potentially most disastrous. All the columns or the whole spreadsheet should be selected before sorting; otherwise only selected columns are sorted, thus mismatching and destroying the data set. If that happens, the sort command should be undone if possible, or the spreadsheet should be closed without saving.

Two keys or columns should be used in sorting into the IRLs: primarily by item number, and secondarily by the response column itself. Sorting by item number is obvious, but sorting by responses is less intuitive but still useful. Identical responses would appear next to each other, so they can be rated all at once. More importantly, the IDs are not in the same order in each IRL, thus enhancing the independence of item ratings, as discussed earlier. In addition, if the ID of 0 was set up as just described, the stem will appear as the first item in each IRL. Macro SortIRL can perform this task. Macro SortID will sort the spreadsheet back by ID and within each ID by item number.

Items 27 and 36 have separate rating manuals for men and women, so each of them needs to be resorted primarily by gender and secondarily by response. After the sorting, only the response column (or columns, if more than one column was used to house long responses) needs to be printed for rating.

Entering the Raters' Ratings.   Sometimes a response resembles two or more categories, which can all be typed into the second column.

In the column for final E-level item rating, use an "IF" function to find all rows that have different ratings in Columns E1 and E2. In Excel, the function would be "=if(rc[-4]rc[-2],"?",rc[-4])" (which means that if the two E-level ratings are not the same, then put a question mark in the cell, otherwise just keep the value given by the first rater). Sorting the spreadsheet by this column would group together only the responses that need to be discussed. Select only these lines and sort them by item number, E-level, and category (of either the first or second rater). A printed copy of this section is given to the two raters before the discussion. Many items can be resolved without a discussion when one rater sees the other's ratings.

After the discussion, the agreed or final item ratings are entered into the last empty column, before the response column. Only the E-level is entered.

Calculating TPRs.   Two TPRs can be calculated. The Macro TPR copies the ratings per protocol from Column 8 (with column heading "EF" in our example), puts them in Column 11 (ogive) and sorts them in descending order. Then the macro calculates a TPR based on the ogive in Column 11 and puts this ogive TPR in Column 12, on the line of the first response. It also computes an item sum and puts it in the next row in Column 12, plus the TPR based on this item sum in the next row in the same column (see Fig. 6.2).

m	1	1	4	a	4	a	4	he may be shy		6	E4	Ogive TPR
m	1	2	4	f	5	a	5	takes patience		6	153	Item Sum TPR
m	1	3	4	b	4	b	4	I put up with it		6	E4	Item Sum

FIG. 6.2. The results of the TPR macro.

Chapter 7
Ego Development as a Stage–Type Theory and a Process

Jane Loevinger
Washington University

with assistance of
Vicki Carlson
Washington University

P. Michiel Westenberg
Leiden University, the Netherlands

Harry Lasker
Independent Consultant, Cambridge, MA

Stage and type theories of character development have a long lineage, going back at least as far as Plato's *Republic.* For a long while they fell into disrepute among psychologists, in part because so many people seemed to lie between stages rather than fitting exactly any stage. Recently, there have again been a number of stage and type theories proposed, in part because the strictly behavioristic psychometric alternatives failed to capture something of the dynamics of character development. Piaget's work on stages of cognitive development also provided new stimulus.

The scoring code for the SCT of ego development illustrates both a contemporary stage–type theory and the kind of problems that have plagued such theories. As detailed in chapter 1, we began classifying sentence completions into a simple four-stage "I-level" system, but in response to needs and suggestions for intermediate ratings by colleagues doing the ratings, the system became more elaborate. Because of the insertion of intermediate stages, ad hoc, it was unclear exactly how many stages there were. That depended on which of the intermediate stages were counted. What is far worse, many of the users of the WUSCT assigned their own numbers to our stages, thus hampering communication of results between users. Furthermore, all attempts to determine whether there is a way to distinguish stages from transitions between stages failed. The original criterion for a stage, that it requires a new vocabulary to describe it, has not been improved on. Such were the problems addressed by our proposal of a new E-level code (see Table 1.1).

The focus of this project in general and of the present book in particular is on measurement of the progress of ego or character development. However, along the way, comparison of the sentence completions of persons of successive stages has yielded a few insights into the possible sources of growth in individuals. Surely, such insights are among the aims of a project like this in the long run.

There are also more direct sources of such knowledge, derived from attempts to assist children or adults to rise on the scale of ego development, and from observation of the transitional process.

Although we have endeavored to evolve a conception of ego development as an abstraction that will apply in every context, in fact, necessarily, each of the studies that has contributed to our work has taken place in some particular context.

We need to consider how the contexts of our studies may have affected our results, and to what extent the limitations can be transcended or accommodated in theory.

In order to find cases at the earliest stages, to balance the emphasis on students and mothers' groups, our early studies sometimes recruited subjects from clinics, prisons, or military units, places where a wider range of people could be found.

In going from measurement of mothers' and other young women's attitudes about problems of family life to measuring the more general characteristic called *ego development,* by means of sentence completions, we needed to find a first approximation to a scale for scoring the SCT.

That first scale was borrowed from a study of stages of "interpersonal integration" of delinquent youths (C. Sullivan et al., 1957). As the term *interpersonal integration* suggests, it was based on the developmental scheme of H. Sullivan's (1953) interpersonal theory of psychiatry. In the study of delinquent adolescent boys, the transitional level from Preconformist (I-2) to Conformist (I-3) was denoted as "I-3 cons"

The label *cons* connoted deception and taking advantage of others, as in the expression "confidence man." The negative connotations of cons did not fit the study of young women, so we sought other ways to designate the transition.

Drawing from another system, stages of interpersonal relatability (Isaacs, 1956), we adopted the code term *Delta* and some of Isaacs' description of the persons and responses at that stage.

A problem in studying the lower stages by the means we chose, namely, reconstruction from adult and adolescent exemplars, was that the lower stage subjects tended to come from a different socioeconomic range than the median stage or high stage subjects. The obvious recourse was to study younger subjects from the same socioeconomic range as the college students and mothers' groups we began with. By the time we were committed to use of the SCT as our instrument of study, the use of young children became problematic. McCammon (1981) tried using an oral presentation of the SCT as a way to overcome children's unfamiliarity with that kind of task. Contrary to our expectation, even sixth-grade school children got higher scores on a written than on an oral SCT.

A few other studies, such as those of Blasi (1976), have used the SCT with young children, but we never had enough cases to provide a basis for a major rethinking of the earliest stages in terms of children's responses.

Many studies using other more age-appropriate instruments have portrayed the early stages of character development in more benign terms than this manual does. Blasi (1984), for example, found spontaneous altruism in many very young children.

A summary of several different approaches to moral and personality development in young children (Loevinger, 1957) reveals another problem. Just as socioeconomic status is a distorting confound in measuring the lower levels among adults, so cognitive immaturity is a possible distorting confound in measuring the lower levels among small children.

At no time was our project tied to a logical definition of the target variable, ego development, or of its successive stages as, for example, Kohlberg's (Colby & Kohlberg, 1987) measure of growth in moral judgment is tied to logically successive perspectives on justice (Blasi, 1998).

Therefore, a logical extension downward was not an option. Our work proceeded entirely empirically. Indeed, it has been criticized by adherents of Piagetian methods because our stages are not strict Piagetian structures. All of our results must be looked at as probabilistic. And because each stage's characteristics are only probabilistic, the line between one stage and the next one is ambiguous.

Some psychologists using the concept of ego development in either research or clinical settings came to have a vivid impression of a level somewhere between the Self-Protective and the Conformist stages. Previously, this intermediate level was called "Delta-3."

In revamping the code from I-level to E-level (see Table 1.1), this level was dropped, among other reasons, because it never had a name. It lacked a name because positive, nameable aspects had not been identified.

The transition from the I-level code to the E-level code was made easier because stage names did not change; however, because this stage or intermediate level, or transitional level did not have a name, it was dropped.

The new simplified E-level code does not have intermediate stages. It has been said that "every classification is an injustice." That is the weakness that has plagued every coding scheme: The code can become a straightjacket.

Inevitably there will be disagreements among raters whether a given response or a given protocol should be called Stage X or Stage X+1. Intermediate ratings arose in part as a way to compromise such disagreements, but in part because of a genuine conviction that there were positive indications of an intermediate standing, possibly marking a process of transition. Over time, some of those intermediate ratings were recognized as stages. The clearest case is the Self-Aware stage (E-5), which began as intermediate between conformity and the conscientious stage.

In order to provide for rating such responses when computing Item Sum Scores (ISS), without complicating the E-level code, we propose to code them as decimals (i.e., E-3.5 for the rating between E-3 and E-4). However, it is preferable to remain with the E-level code as presented in Table 1.1, keeping in mind that the number of stages is arbitrary, as are also the boundaries of each stage.

As the SCT has been applied in many new contexts (see chapter 8), new insights into the earliest stages have resulted.

Westenberg (1998) devised an SCT for Dutch children and tested thousands of cases, in constructing his own scoring manual, by a process paralleling the one detailed in this volume. As we had anticipated, a more positive image of the earliest stages emerged.

In a different context, Lasker (1978) studied adults on the Island of Curaçao in the Netherlands Antilles. Remarkably, about one third of the adult population of Curaçao were at the stage then called Delta-3 (now E-3.5).

Both the individual's adjustment and the possibility of a society depend on at least minimal capacity for conformity. In the long history of theories of character development, Conformity is the stage and type most often clearly recognized, both as an achievement and as a condition for social existence, and, less often, as a constraint on further character development.

Businesses on the island of Curaçao hired Lasker to conduct training sessions with their employees, with the aim of raising ego levels. Lasker's subjects, men, mostly between 25 and 35 years, and of varying socioeconomic levels and ethnic groups, were first tested with an early version of the SCT, then sorted into training groups on the basis of their level.

The most successful of the training groups was that aimed at raising people of the Delta-3 (now E-3.5) group to the Conformist level, (E4). It is understandable that group activity would encourage rising to the Conformist level, and it is also understandable that businesses would have a stake in their employees rising to that level.

Lasker was impressed by the distinctiveness of the group between Self-Protective and Conformist, perhaps because of the coincidence of ego levels, social class, and occupational status on the island where he worked. The situation is hauntingly reminiscent of Plato's Republic, except that Plato did not anticipate the ethnic differences that mark the classes on Curaçao.

Because Lasker recorded the spoken interactions of his subjects in the training sessions, they provide a uniquely valuable source of insight into the transitional process. Some of his observations are recorded here, not as a definition of a new level, but as a first glimpse of a transitional process.

At E-3.5, compared to E-3, the person is more aware of the presence of others, and particularly of their approval or disapproval, and possible respect. However, at E-3.5, the subject does not see others as having their own motives and inner life. Furthermore, at E-3.5, the preoccupation of the E-3 subject with dominating or being dominated is deflected to dominating the person's own impulses, which is effortful.

Behaving oneself is an important theme of the SCTs at this level. Good behavior is defined almost entirely in terms of prohibited acts rather than in terms of positively valued behaviors. For example, "Rules are— for you not to do things in front of children."

Hostility may be disguised or displaced, such as saying that "troublemakers should be eliminated."

The E-3 desire to dominate may be somewhat modulated, "A husband has a right to—" "rule his home," or "get what he wants from his wife."

As compared to the E-3 subject, however, for whom rules may be arbitrary impositions, the E-3.5 has a greater capacity to recognize rules, and their application to everyone. However, rules mostly cover specific behaviors, like "be on time at work."

At the same time, "rules are everywhere in this world, for example, traffic rules."

Although impulse control and respect for rules are advanced over that of the E-3 level, they remain effortful and not easily, or automatically integrated, as they are at the E-4 and higher levels.

A prominent theme at E-3.5 is respect. The person earns respect by behaving, and thus being respected by others. That helps establish his or her own self-respect. The self-respect is based on something real, like behaving oneself or finishing tasks.

Impulsive level people can lack all self-esteem, or can engage in braggadocio. The E-3.5 subject "just can't stand people who brag a lot."

Lasker's observations, in contrast to Westenberg's, do not alter the pictures of the Self-Protective and Conformist stages drawn in the present and the original scoring manuals of the SCT. Most of the characteristics that Lasker ascribed to the E-3.5 level are easily classified as either Self-Protective (E-3) or Conformist (E-4) by the present manual or by Westenberg's Dutch manual. The data of Westenberg and his colleagues, based on thousands of Dutch youths, agree with our data that there is not a true stage between the Self-Protective and the Conformist levels. The major interest in Lasker's observations is that the group interactions give a glimpse of the process of change.

The support of the group gives some self-acceptance, at the same time that the person learns to accept others, thus to acknowledge that differences of opinions do not automatically signify unacceptability or rejection.

The safety of the group permits examination of individual feelings, such as hostilities, that would be unacceptable if expressed in direct actions. That opens the way to acknowledging and naming—at least to oneself—other personal feelings. That leads, in turn, to recognizing corresponding feelings in others.

Empathy with others in the group lays the basis for adopting the norm of reciprocity, a characteristic of the E-4 person. Empathy and self-acceptance lead to the thoughts that "I am like other people," "I want other people to like me," "I can choose to be more like other people." "I would like to be part of the (or a) group"is the most characteristic E-4 stance.

Studies such as Westenberg's and Lasker's illustrate new directions that the theory can lead to, such as study of new and different populations and study of the process of change Hauser, Powers, and Noam (1991).

We recommend that for the present, workers use the E-level code as it has been presented in this volume, without interpolating stages such as E-3.5. However, given the arbitrary nature of every codification, the possibility will always be open for further insights.

In conclusion, when the early stages of ego development are studied in children passing through the stages in normal time, a more positive and benign picture of the early stages emerges than when the early stages are reconstructed from adolescents or adults. That is now well established in the United States and Holland. A theoretical explanation can be found in H. Sullivan (1953). In his account of the early developmental stages, he identified as a "malevolent transformation" what may happen to a child when rebuffed or ridiculed when manifesting a need for tenderness. The child may adopt the attitude that he or she is living in a world of enemies. That attitude will at least partially arrest further development. By this reasoning the negative attitudes of the Preconformist levels in adolescents and adults are a result of their negative reactions to some wounding emotional experiences in childhood, combined with the consequent arrested ego development.

Hauser et al. (1991) studied the process of ego development in the most naturalistic setting imaginable, in the interactions of adolescent boys and girls with their parents. They gave SCTs to a large number of adolescents and their parents, and selected representative groups for study. Their prototypical experiment put an adolescent and his or her parents in a room. They then gave them a moral dilemma, of the kind used in Kohlberg's test of moral judgment, and requested that the family agree on a solution. The family interactions were recorded verbatim. The key words for Hauser et al. are *constraining* and *enabling*. A parent who ignores or ridicules or brushes aside the child's suggestions is constraining the child from developing individuality and his or her own ideas. In contrast, a parent who pays attention to the child's suggestions, replies to them seriously, without belittling, or who expresses appreciation for the child's participation, is enabling the child to grow. Hauser et al. listed many specific ways of constraining and enabling.

Parents who themselves have a relatively high ego level are more likely to reply to their children with enabling and encouragement, whereas parents with relatively low ego level are in general more likely to make constraining remarks. Because the enabling remarks encourage the child's individuality and other characteristics of higher ego levels, Hauser et al. proposed here a theory of how ego level is transmitted.

Hauser and his colleagues studied the process of ego development in another sense too. Their study was longitudinal and, moreover, they found examples of different trajectories, including adolescents who were steady conformists, some who were regularly accelerated in their ego development, and others who were profoundly arrested.

Chapter 8
Cross-Cultural Applications of the WUSCT

Vicki Carlson
Washington University
P. Michiel Westenberg
Leiden University, the Netherlands

The Washington University Sentence Completion Test (WUSCT) has been translated into at least 11 other languages to allow its inclusion in research conducted in languages other than English (see Table 8.1). Translated versions of the WUSCT have been used to examine the relationship between ego development and achievement motivation and economic development (Lasker, 1978), models of achievement in women (von der Lippe, 1988), professional training activities (Limoges, 1980; Paul, 1980), the effects of trauma (Zlotogorski, 1985), delinquency (Tochio & Akiba, 1988; Tochio & Hanada, 1991), personality correlates of corporate subcultures (Kusatsu, 1977), the subcultural aspects of academic disciplines (Costa & Campos, 1987), religion and caste (Dhruvarajan, 1981), fluency among bilinguals (Hy, 1986), moral and social values (Snarey & Blasi, 1980), and psychosocial process correlates of various psychiatric diagnostic groups (Kapfhammer, Neumeier, & Scherer, 1993).

Documentation of cross-cultural differences was rarely the primary focus of these studies. However, linguistic and cultural differences are described in this literature. They are mentioned in method sections as they relate to translation or to adaptations necessary for implementation in other settings. Cultural issues sometimes are elaborated in more detail in discussion sections as authors consider results that differ from patterns found in research conducted in English. A few investigators have addressed cultural differences directly and some have included rich ethnographic, historical, religious, and economic detail differences in patterns of WUSCT

TABLE 8.1
Examples of Published Studies That Have Used a Translation of the WUSCT

Language	Country, Setting	Sample Characteristics	Author	Date	Study Questions
Dutch	The Netherlands	2,773 8- to 25-year-olds; 544 were psychiatric outpatients; 2,229 were a representative comparison sample	Westenberg et al.	1998	■ How does a large sample of normal 8- to 25-year-olds perform on a Dutch version of the WUSCT scored with a Dutch manual? ■ How does a sample of psychiatric outpatients compare with a comparison group on the SCT for youth?
Dutch	Curaçao, Netherlands Antilles	61 of 380 subjects chose to complete the SCT in Dutch	Lasker	1978	■ See Lasker (1978) under Papiamentu
French	Canada	32 nurses	Paul	1979, 1980	■ What is the ego development level among community health nurses?
French	Canada	32 high school students in a vocational school	Limoges	1979, 1980	■ What is the relationship between ego development and high school students' "vocational maturity"?
German	Germany	139 17- to 26-year-olds with psychiatric disorders; 100 comparison subjects	Kapfhammer et al.	1993	■ What is the relationship between ego development and psychiatric disorders?
Hebrew	Israel, Kibbutz	42 male and female: 11 60- to 67-year-old Kibbutz "founders"; 11 55- to 72-year-old long-term members; 9 27- to 42-year-old kibbutz-born members; and 11 17- to 33-year-old kibbutz-born youth	Snarey & Blasi	1980	■ Would founders, long-term residents, and members born into kibbutz communities differ on ego level ? ■ Does the English manual serve to rate Hebrew responses?
Hebrew or English	Israel	73 male and female adult offspring of Holocaust survivors and 68 male and female comparison subjects	Zlotogorski	1985	■ Are there differences in ego level, as measured by SCT, that would support a child-of-survivor syndrome?
Japanese	Japan	158 female adolescents attending junior and senior high schools; 49 female adolescents in reformatories	Katō	1981	■ Do delinquent adolescent girls have lower ego levels as measured by the WUSCT?

Japanese	Japan	295 men, a minimum of 10 from each of 19 professional levels in Matsumoto, city of 150,000 on Honshu-mainland	Kusatsu	1977, 1978	• Comparison of Japanese scores with American • Does an analysis of response content inform our understanding of Japanese national character? • Is ego level related to "occupational culture"?
Japanese	Japan	270 14- to 24-year-old females, most were middle class, all lived in Tokyo or Sariama	Sasaki	1981a	• How does a representative sample of Japanese adolescent girls score on the WUSCT?
Japanese	Japan	610 men aged 30 to 59 years, representative sample of men in Tokyo, drawn from voting records	Sasaki	1981b	• How does a representative sample of Japanese men score on the WUSCT?
Japanese	Japan	100 female delinquents ages 13 to 19; 180 female comparisons ages 15 to 18	Tochio & Hanada	1991	• Is there evidence for "humiliation of the ego" in the content of Conformist and Postconformist protocols? • Are ego levels of female delinquents similar to those of same-aged comparison females?
Japanese	Japan	612 normal male and female Japanese 10- to 70-year-olds	Watanabe & Yamamoto	1989	• Are ego levels of a broad range of Japanese individuals similar to those reported for adults in the U.S.?
Kanada	India	23 Brahmin and 23 Vokkaglia women, living in a rural village in southern India	Dhnvarajan	1981	• Do SCT scores vary by caste? • How does response content relate to cultural, religious, social, and economic issues?

(continued)

59

TABLE 8.1
(continued)

Norwegian	Norway	von der Lippe	33 mother–daughter pairs, ranging in age from 19 to 69 years	1988	•What are the relationships among occupational, educational, and social achievement in women and what are the socialization and ego development processes associated with differing emphases placed on the various types of achievement?
Papiamentu	Curaçao, Netherlands Antilles	Lasker	80 male pilot subjects; 380 males, 25 to 35 years old, sample representative of three SES levels in seven industries	1978	▪ Can the SCT, developed with U.S. females, successfully assess ego level in Curaçaoan men?
			118 subjects chose to complete SCT in Papiamentu, a language unique to Curaçao		▪ Are Curaçaoan responses psychometrically comparable to U.S. responses?
Portuguese	Portugal	Costa & Campos	250 male and female 18- to 23-year-olds, all second-year university students	1987	▪ Is it useful to group trainees in need achievement workshops by ego level? ▪ Are there systematic differences in ego level related to students' choice of major academic discipline?
Sinhalese or Tami?	Sri Lanka	Weathersby		1993	▪ What is the relationship between ego level and leadership conceptualizations?
Vietnamese	United States	Hy	84 male and female 13- to 28-year-old Vietnamese refugees living in two midwestern U.S. cities	1986	▪ How does the language of administration affect ego development scores among young bilingual (Vietnamese/ English) refugees? ▪ Does the content of the refugees' responses suggest cultural differences?

scores. In addition, the English version of the WUSCT has been used to explore cross-cultural questions with culturally and ethnically diverse subpopulations in English-speaking countries (see Table 8.2). Studies in English are not discussed. The following discussion is restricted to non-English uses of the WUSCT.

This chapter is not an attempt to evaluate the claims concerning cross-cultural differences in ego development as measured by the WUSCT. Rather, it is an effort to inform the reader of the international uses of the measure and an attempt to highlight methodological issues relevant to effective transplantation to another setting of a personality assessment system developed in the United States for use with native English speakers. These issues, considered along with descriptions of research on the international applications of other psychological measures can inform the ways we continue the examination of cross-cultural differences in ego development in the future.

THE FIRST TRANSLATION OF THE WUSCT

Curaçao, the WUSCT, and Economic Development. The first translations of the WUSCT were into Dutch and Papiamentu (a local language derived from Dutch) for use on Curaçao, the largest island in the Netherlands Antilles, off the west coast of Colombia. The motivation for that study originated in an economic development program in rural India during the 1960s. Lasker, a Harvard undergraduate, served as a trainer in an experimental economic development program that was based on David McClelland's achievement motivation theories. The intent was to increase worker's "need achievement," which would result in increased economic success for graduates of the program. The U.S. team conducted intensive training workshops that produced significant change for some participants, but not for others. An unexpected finding was that the level of training effectiveness could be predicted from images the participants presented in Thematic Apperception Test (TAT) protocols collected prior to the training. Individuals whose achievement motivation increased with training told stories with images of "personal efficacy" such as active problem solving, autonomy, and goal directedness. Individuals who did not change with training could be characterized by cognitive simplicity, a lack of interest in achievement thinking, an apathetic sense of fatalism, limited abilities in considering the future, planning ahead, or realistically setting goals. Their levels of education were lower. They were rated as hostile and suspicious of others' motives and worked poorly in groups. The researchers named this pattern *low personal efficacy.*

Not long after returning from the India project, Lasker learned of Loevinger's recently published account of ego development stages and the related assessment technique, the WUSCT. He was struck by the similarity between the low personal efficacy pattern his team had discovered in India and Loevinger's descriptions of Preconformist stages. Lasker saw in the WUSCT the potential for an efficient

TABLE 8.2
Examples of Studies Addressing Cross-Cultural Issues That Have Used the WUSCT in English

Language	Country Setting	Sample Characteristics	Author	Date	Study Questions
English	Australia and India	81 male and 90 female Australian students; 55 male and 55 female college students from one of five universities in Madras, India	Ravinder	1986	• Does the model of ego development stages as measured by the WUSCT apply to both Australian and Indian young adult populations?
English	United States, Boston, MA	30 immigrants, 23 U.S.-born high school students, male and female. Immigrants represented 13 different ethnic backgrounds	Arredondo-Dowd	1981	• What are the psychological characteristics of adolescents who have experienced immigration? • Would a developmental intervention have an impact on ego development level?
English	United States, Boston, MA	17 male and female adolescent immigrants	Arredondo	1984	• What is the impact of an intervention program on moral reasoning and ego development in a population of young immigrants?
English	United States, Haight-Ashbury District, San Francisco, CA	32 males, 26 females, 16 to 35 years of age	Haan & Stroud	1973	• Are moral and ego development characteristics different within a subculture defined by adherence to moral utopian principles?
English	United States, New Haven, CT	52 Puerto Rican, 20 Black, and 32 White male opiod addicts	Wurzman, Rounsaville, & Kleber	1983	• Are there subcultural differences in response content on the WUSCT that might contribute to the tailoring of drug intervention srtaegies to make them more in alignment with cultural values?
English	United States, urban east coast, major university	193 Black undergraduates	Dunston & Roberts	1987	• What are the interrelationships among ego development, moral judgment, self-concept, and political–social values in a Black college-age population?
English	United States, urban, midsouth, universities	30 male and 30 female Black undergraduates	Looney	1988	• What is the relationship between ego development and Black identity formation?

screening tool that could allow training activities to be adapted to fit the needs of different groups of trainees. The opportunity to test the value of screening with the WUSCT soon presented itself.

McClelland's training programs in India and other underdeveloped areas received considerable press coverage. In 1969, the government of Curaçao, spurred by workers' unrest due to rapid economic changes in oil and other industries, invited McClelland's training team, which again included Lasker, to conduct achievement motivation trainings. Lasker, then a graduate student, used the opportunity to screen the trainees for ego level, as measured by the WUSCT.

This practical application of the WUSCT on Curaçao was the first, and one of the most methodologically extensive, cross-cultural applications of the WUSCT. Respondents were offered the choice of responding in Dutch, Papiamentu, or English. Responses were translated into English for rating by expert coders. The test was piloted with 80 men and then used with the study sample of 380 males selected to represent three socioeconomic status (SES) levels in seven different industries. Reliability and validity were examined and extensive attention was paid to the psychometric properties of the scores. Lasker appreciated Loevinger's emphasis on the interplay between theory and empirical findings and implemented Loevinger's psychometric methods of microvalidation to evaluate the data collected in Curaçao, reviewing the spread of scores on each item and checking individual item response scores against total protocol ratings (TPRs). In addition, because published WUSCT manuals had only been validated for use with women, he produced rating manuals for the eight sentence stems Loevinger and her colleagues had recently developed for use with men.

Differentiating Preconformist from Conformist levels was critical to Lasker's screening needs, so he found it useful to elaborate on the rating system for what was then called the Delta-3 transitional substage. Selfprotective responses were also considerably more prevalent on Curaçao. One third of the respondents were rated at this level. Postconformist stages were less prevalent. Lasker described historical and economic issues that he considered the reasons for such different patterns of scores on the island. Lasker's study demonstrated that screening for ego level was an effective way to tailor training content to individual characteristics.

Reflecting on the relevance of the Curaçao findings to the question of "universality" of ego development theory and the WUSCT method, Lasker (1978) cautioned that Curaçao is a

completely Western society which is especially urban and industrialized.... Evidence of the ego continuum from traditional, non-western societies is still to be collected. Some rightfully question whether the end point of development in the ego scheme, the integrated self, would be the same in a society with less heavy value emphasis on individual development. (p. 45)

Subsequent studies, some of them conducted by sociologists like Lasker, have employed the WUSCT in non-Western societies. They offer insights into the question he asked.

STUDIES OF EGO DEVELOPMENT
IN NON-WESTERN SOCIETIES

Ego Development and the Japanese Character.   The first researcher to use the WUSCT in Japan was Kusatsu (1977, 1978). He provided extensive descriptions of variation in ego development scores as they related to cultural and corporate subcultural differences.

Kusatsu's study employed direct measures of personality, and interpersonal characteristics in a sample stratified by occupation. He demonstrated considerable diversity among individuals, findings that contradicted previous oversimplifications of Japanese "cultural identity." His sample included 295 men in Matsumoto, a city of 170,000 on Honshu mainland. They were systematically drawn from jobs at 19 professional levels. Data collection included an adapted, 12-item version of the WUSCT, measures of attitudes, values, interpersonal orientation, political orientation, Inkeles' conception of modernity, and life satisfaction. WUSCT responses were first rated with Loevinger et al.'s (1970) English manual. Internal consistency was similar to that reported for U.S. samples.

After a review of the correspondence of individual item ratings as compared to TPRs, adjustments were made to the coding system for about 15% to 20% of the responses. Revisions of scoring were intended to maintain the intent of the coding system, especially as a method of documenting conformity and the emergence from it. For example,

> One noticeable example of difference between Japanese and American responses is found for the stub of the sentence completions: "The thing I like about myself is...." Such responses as "nothing at all" or "something in myself with which I am dissatisfied" were rated at the transitional stage (I 3/4) between Conformity and Conscientious stages, through some of them are rated at the Impulsive stage (I 2) in Loevinger's manual. This is because of the Japanese norm of humiliation of the individual ego. (Kusatsu, 1977, p. 66)

As in the United States, Japanese subjects' ego levels varied predictably with demographic characteristics such as occupational prestige ($r = .42$), and education ($r = .43$). More urban experience and fathers' education level were associated with the highest ego scores. In contrast with U.S. findings of stability throughout adulthood, Kusatsu interpreted age-related patterns in scores as suggestive of continued change in ego development over the course of adult life in response to characteristics of the workplace and one's position in it. Longitudinal research would be required to test this hypothesis drawn from age-difference patterns in a cross-sectional study.

Kusatsu evaluated response content to consider claims about the Japanese character. While affirming the structural similarity of Preconformist, Conformist, and Postconformist levels of ego functioning between Japanese and U.S. samples, he described variation in the preoccupations or content of the Conformist and Postconformist Japanese responses. Japanese conformists' responses were characterized by a constant awareness of others and a naturalistic conception of social role. Japanese Postconformist responses were characterized by efforts to transcend socially prescribed roles, the emergence of a selfhood, desires for achievement, abstract and complex ideas of self and society, and active commitment to the society based on a sense of identity that emerges out of a resolution of conflict between self and society (Kusatsu, 1978).

Studies Directed at Adapting the WUSCT for Use in Japan.   Sasaki (1980) reviewed the initial uses of the WUSCT in Japan. Miyashita and Uechi (1981, 1983), reporting on studies of reliability and validity of the WUSCT in Japan, noted the need for some minor changes in items to address sociocultural issues. Other investigators have noted the need to change or drop particular items or wordings and have described efforts to make scoring appropriate for Japanese responses. Kato (1981) made a Japanese translation of Loevinger's coding manual for use in Japan. Sasaki (1981a, 1981b) constructed a Japanese manual by using the psychometric principles Loevinger and her colleagues employed in constructing the original English manual.

Several Japanese studies are especially valuable due to their large, representative samples. Watanabe and Yamamoto (1989) translated and adapted the WUSCT for use with 612 male and female subjects, ages 10 to 70 years olds. Substantial adaptations were made to the items included in the Japanese WUSCT prior to its use in normative studies. Nine items were eliminated. Items concerning sex were considered inappropriate for the youngest of their subjects and were dropped. In addition, items specific to male and female versions of the test were eliminated. Others were dropped because responses to them failed to produce an adequate range of scores. Such adaptations need to be born in mind when considering comparisons with results in other countries.

Sasaki (1981b) used a modified Japanese WUSCT with 610 male adults ranging in age from 30 to 59 years. Subjects were randomly drawn from voting files in Tokyo. As in the United States, ego level was not related to age in adulthood. Evidence for culture-specific variation in response content concerning the nature of the self, especially in its relationship with the community was examined. Sasaki suggested some of the differences previously described may be due to language differences and resulting confusion, especially for items in which the respondent has to express a thought concerning the self. In a separate study, Sasaki (1981a) implemented the SCT with middle-class adolescent girls. In conducting these studies, Sasaki again found that some adaptations in item content were necessary.

In order to explore hypotheses concerning immature ego development as a contributor to female adolescent delinquency, Tochio and Akiba (1988) and Tochio and Hanada (1991) employed the Japanese WUSCT. They used Sasaki's (1981a, 1981b) Japanese manual for scoring.

Personality and Women's Caste Membership in Rural India. In an ethnographically rich account of research using the WUSCT to study caste differences in a sample of 46 women in her village of origin, Dhruvarajan (1981) emphasized the role of cultural and religious values in shaping ego level. She used an oral presentation of the WUSCT in Kanada, the language of the area. She reported few instances of Postconformist ego level among her 46 respondents and discussed the findings in terms of the powerful religious, social, economic, and interpersonal pressures toward dependency that she described as the normative context for women in this culture. The setting was rural, income and education were relatively low, and the sample was too small to support a conclusion that cultural differences existed beyond the influence of SES and the lack of "modernizing influences" found in more urban settings. Yet, Dhruvarajan's detailed descriptions of women's life in this setting offer Western readers an opportunity to consider genuinely different characterizations of "the self."

A strength of this study was the use of history, anthropology, and ethnographic methods to describe the religious and social context of life in the village. Dhruvarajan illustrated how deeply the meaning of "self" and self in relationship to others are embedded in caste, gender relations, and religion. The value a woman places on her "self" varies tremendously with her caste status, her marital status, and the gender of her children. Dhruvarajan described the influence of Hindu religion in everyday life especially the attention required in monitoring the potential for ritual "pollution" she might cause others by improper behavior. This study illustrated relationships between psychological processes and religion, an issue rarely included in psychological research published in the West. In this and other WUSCT studies in other settings, investigators have introduced features of religious life in an effort to account for patterns in ego levels or response content.

WUSCT STUDIES IN LANGUAGES OTHER THAN ENGLISH IN WESTERN SOCIETIES

Ego Development As a Measure of Psychological Change in Canada. Paul (1979, 1980) employed a French translation of the WUSCT with a sample of 32 nurses in Quebec. They were participating in an 8-week training program aimed at increasing their participation in counseling activities. Ego level was assessed before and after the training for descriptive purposes. There was no significant change in ego level related to this brief training and an increase had not been specifically predicted by the researchers. Paul endorsed the applicability of the measure in this setting. Responses to the French version of the WUSCT were reliably rated ($r = .80$) by bilingual raters who used the English manual to rate the French responses.

Limoges (1980) used a French WUSCT in a training study conducted with 32 high school students in Montreal. Half of the students were participating in a semester-long course aimed at vocational and career-related aspects of psychological maturity. Students in the experimental group demonstrated a significant increase in ego development scores from pretest to posttest, however, there was no comparable increase in the measure of career maturity as measured by the Professional Development Inventory (PDI). WUSCT scores and PDI scores were not correlated before or after the intervention.

Ego Development and Academic Subcultures in Portugal. Costa and Campos (1987) used a Portuguese translation to explore the relationship between ego level and primary area of study in a university setting. The subjects were 250 males and females, ages 18 to 23. All of the subjects were in their second year of study in law, engineering, medicine, economics, and the arts. In general, females were rated at higher ego levels than males. There was no main effect of area of study, however, there was a gender by field-of-study interaction. In engineering, the males had higher ratings than females. Among men, students in law and engineering attained the highest scores and students in economics and arts scored the lowest. The authors urged further study before making conclusions. SES variables were not included in analyses and may have played a role in the differences that were observed.

Ego Development and Psychopathology in Germany. Kapfhammer et al. (1993) used the WUSCT to compare a psychiatric population of young adults (ages 17–26; $N = 139$) with a group of their age peers without psychopathology (ages 17–26; $N = 100$). Consistent with expectations, the psychiatric population scored significantly lower in terms of ego development. Within the psychiatric sample, ego development was unrelated to the prevalence of the different psychiatric disorders; to a general measure of ego strength; to a self-concept measure; and to the success of psychosocial adjustment. The authors concluded that ego development is not associated with subjective well-being or social adjustment.

The authors did not describe their translation methods nor did they comment on the applicability of the U.S. scoring manual in a German sample.

Ego Development and Context in Israel. Snarey and Blasi (1980) translated the WUSCT into Hebrew in order to test hypotheses about ego levels and various levels of experience with the Kibbutz system. They predicted that the individuals who came to Israel in the 1930s to establish "just communities" and had spent decades trying to implement their ideals, would operate at higher levels than individuals who came later or were born into the system. Their hypotheses were affirmed, however, experience in the kibbutz was completely confounded by age, leaving the finding less robust. In addition, Snarey and Blasi (1980) reported very few individuals, even the young ones, at the Self-Protective level. They suggested that kibbutz values serve to produce fewer individuals who are at this level as adults or that life in the kibbutz holds the Self-Protective stance in very low esteem and may serve to encourage more culturally acceptable answers.

Another inquiry into the effects of experience on ego level was conducted in Hebrew by Zlotogorski (1985). He used the WUSCT to test 73 adult children of holocaust survivors for indications of a child-of-survivor syndrome. Sixty-eight men and women served as comparison subjects. Results did not support such a syndrome as measured by differences in ego development.

Vietnamese Immigrants in the United States: A Bilingual Assessment of Ego Development.   Hy (1986) directly explored language influences by administering half the WUSCT items in English and half in Vietnamese with a sample of bilingual refugees. In a within-subjects design, he compared subsets of scores for items administered in each language and found them comparable. High and low scores appeared equally in both languages indicating no bias with either English or Vietnamese. Ego level was related to language fluency. When individuals were substantially more fluent in one language, ego level was higher for items administered in the favored language. Subjects with relatively less fluent Vietnamese omitted more responses to stems in Vietnamese than they did to English stems.

Responses were rated by a Vietnamese/English bilingual who used Vietnamese responses and the English manual. Reliability was established with an English-speaking rater who responded to English translations of the Vietnamese responses. Reliabilities were very similar for responses made in Vietnamese, $r = .75$ and those made in English, $r = .76$.

In addition to the focus on language in WUSCT research, Hy's study exemplifies the growing complexity of studying cross-cultural differences. The sample of young Vietnamese refugees—influenced by centuries-old Southeast Asian traditions including the teachings of Confucious, living in the United States, speaking Vietnamese and English, and practicing Catholicism—represent many cultural influences. The geographic and communicative isolation that helped establish different languages and cultural practices over the centuries, is rapidly diminishing.

CONTINUING THE DEVELOPMENT
OF THE WUSCT METHOD AND THEORY

Mapping Ego Development During Childhood and Adolescence: The Netherlands.   Both the first translation of the WUSCT (Lasker, 1978) and the most recent one (Westenberg, Jonckheer, & Treffers, in press; see also chapter 10, this volume) have been in Dutch. The central purpose of the more recent study was to compare a psychiatric, outpatient population of children and adolescents (ages 8–18) with a large and representative sample of school children without major pathology. In the several phases of the project, more than 2,500 WUSCT protocols were assembled, for which a Dutch scoring manual had to be developed. In the process of making the Dutch manual, the investigators were faced with the question of whether Loevinger's developmental model and scoring manual were directly applicable to children and adolescents. In fact, the first task was to develop a new version of the WUSCT suitable for children and adolescents (see chapter 10, this volume). This study was the first systematic attempt to develop a scoring manual for children and adolescents.

The U.S. samples used in developing (Loevinger & Wessler, 1970) and revising (Hy & Loevinger, 1996) the WUSCT consisted primarily of (young) adults, with the large majority being older than 18. Loevinger and her colleagues never described these samples as "representative" nor did they claim that the prevalence of ego levels obtained during the measurement development process reflected ego level norms for the United States. In contrast, the samples used to develop the Dutch SCT-Y consisted primarily of children, adolescents, and young adults, with the large majority being younger than 18. Westenberg et al.'s (1998) explicit attempt was to assemble a representative sample of 8- to 18-year-olds, to make the comparison with a psychiatric population of children and adolescents.

Due to the age difference between the U.S. and Dutch samples, the distribution of ego levels differed in predictable ways: The U.S. samples included relatively few Preconformist but many Postconformist subjects, whereas the Dutch samples consisted of relatively few Postconformist but many Preconformist subjects. The sample differences are related to differences in the scoring manuals: The U.S. manual provides much detail in the Postconformist region and less detail in Preconformist region, whereas the Dutch manual provides much detail in the Preconformist region and less detail in the Postconformist region.

This greater detail in the Preconformist region of the Dutch manual was due to additional response categories emerging primarily at the Preconformist levels, and a downshift of response categories placed at the Conformist level in the U.S. manual to the Preconformist levels in the Dutch manual. An example of a downshift is the response category "When I am criticized— *it doesn't bother me.*" It is placed at the Conformist level in the U.S. manual, but it emerged at the Self-Protective level in the Dutch manual (according to the microvalidation procedure, see chapter 1, this volume). Such responses suggest a self-focused form of control aimed at the protection of one's own feelings. In contrast, Loevinger's description of control at the Self-Protective level concentrates on interpersonally malignant forms of control, such as the punitive, manipulative, and exploitative attitude. The Dutch manual for the Preconformist levels generally suggests a more balanced picture of the earliest developmental levels, including both positive and negative elements, at least when referring to the development of the children and adolescents. Results are summarized as offering an overall affirmation of Loevinger's theory with variations in content and emotional tone needed at the first three ego levels. Differences between Dutch and U.S. findings are described as due more to the younger age and representative nature of the sample than due to cultural or language differences. But a definitive verdict on the correct explanation of the differences awaits the completion of a similar project in the United States. Are U.S. youth comparable to Dutch youth in terms of their ego development?

METHODOLOGICAL ISSUES RELEVANT TO WUSCT RESEARCH IN OTHER LANGUAGES

Linguistic Variation and Translating Stems.   Despite the importance of linguistic nuances in item selection, investigators frequently offered little detail on their methods of translating stems. Numerous articles simply state that the WUSCT was translated. Others describe difficulties or mention the number of stems that were dropped from the set. In some cases, users of the English WUSCT have had to make some adjustments when studying a defined subgroup within the larger language community.

The use of multiple translators and systematic evaluation of their translations have been suggested in a number of studies (Dhruvarajan, 1981; Hy 1986; Westenberg et al., chapter 10, this volume). Backward translation, a common technique for checking the adequacy of a translation in which an independent translator translates the translation back into English, offers some benefits and possible drawbacks. For example, Dhruvaragan (1981) used local (rural India) idioms to try to encompass the meanings of original sentence stems in her translation to Kanada. Her goal was to capture the *essence* of the issues addressed in the original stems (including intentional ambiguities), rather than exact translations of the words. Literal English back-translations of the Kanada idioms she used give a glimpse of how very different successful stem translations can be compared to original wordings.

Although the English language offers relatively few ways to encode issues of social standing or other aspects of interpersonal relationships within vocabulary and grammar, other languages operate differently. For example, Hy (personal communication, 1996) described issues that arose in translating the English word "I" into Vietnamese. In Vietnamese, several pronouns indicate the self. Each one contains status and relational information, related to characteristics of the speaker, the addressee, and relationship between them. The common word, *toi,* is the appropriate form for situations in which two adults are speaking together. However, if respondents were to be high school students, *em* is a better translation. It connotes that the addressee is younger than the speaker, and *em* is much more commonly used in that age range than the word *toi.* For even younger subjects in South Vietnam, the word *con* would be the better translation. In Vietnamese, sample characteristics are important in planning the appropriate translation to use.

Hy (1986; see also Appendix F, this volume) focused considerable attention on translation procedures. He suggested conferring with other fluent bilinguals, piloting and revising translations, and seeking feedback from subjects and experts in order to produce the best match in connotation, denotation, and stem complexity.

Translations of Responses for Coding Purposes.   Researchers using the WUSCT in new settings often wish to establish interrater reliability with experienced English-speaking U.S. raters, a step that requires translation of responses originally given in another language into English.

For rating purposes, translation must go beyond conveying the essential referential meaning of the response to include notes concerning the overall meaning of the response. This broader meaning can include context-sensitive phrases, terms that index status hierarchies (e.g., pronouns and kin terms), cliché qualities of certain statements, and allusions to broader cultural domains (e.g., religion and literature). For this purpose, translators must be warned against the strategy of selecting a common American cliché that would convey most of the meaning of a phrase which, as originally stated, would not be sensible to an American listener. That same phrase might be unique, perhaps poetic or insightful to listeners in the original context. To either reduce or elevate a response to an English cliché form could alter ego development relevant information contained in the original response.

Including translation reliability is appropriate. Dhruvarajan (1981) offered the English-speaking trained raters two translations of several stems. This offered a way to attune raters to cultural and language issues in the other culture, however, it would be a less efficient way to rate. With adequate reliability established, she used her own ratings for the analyses, thereby employing her knowledge of the language and the culture in rating her sample's responses. Bilingual raters offer an efficient way to bring knowledge of the respondents' language and culture together with knowledge of ego development theory and assessment skills. It is an approach that has been used by a number of investigators for at least some of their raters.

Two other approaches to using local raters exist: translating the whole manual (Kato, 1981) and constructing a new manual based on responses made by individuals in the new language (Sasaki, 1981a; Westenberg et al., 1998). Trade-offs among time, the perceived need for sensitivity to local language and content, and possible future uses of a translation determine the type of rating system appropriate for a given study.

Administration of the WUSCT in Another Setting.   What does it mean for a "subject" to participate in a study of psychological process. Observant researchers use their knowledge about these norms in designing and interpreting their studies. Details about them are sometimes found in method sections. They may include administration adaptations, a listing of stems dropped due to content deemed inappropriate for public discussion, and comments that were part of standard procedures or instructions given to subjects.

Subjects' experience with and attitudes about social science research may have some influence on responses given. Many studies take place in urban settings near universities where familiarity with research and attitudes toward it may be more similar to those of the U.S. subjects with whom the WUSCT was developed than in rural or underdeveloped settings.

Urbanization, opportunities for education, and experience with diverse groups of people have been shown to be related to higher levels of ego development as measured by the WUSCT. Perhaps other correlates of the urban–nonurban distinction, including aspects of the data collection process itself, also influence response content. Attitudes toward openly sharing information or personal impressions in a research situation vary widely in different settings. Social norms concerning the presentation of self also differ. It is realistic to expect those values to influence the degree to which respondents report thoughts that come to their minds as they complete sentence stems.

EVALUATING, RATING RESPONSES, AND ADAPTING THE SCALE

Reliability.   Having each response rated by two or more raters is the standard procedure. The separate ratings are the basis for reliability estimates. More importantly, two raters can resolve differences and catch inevitable human errors. Multiple raters are even more essential when the WUSCT is conducted in another language. Raters confer on rating categories. When disagreements and subsequent resolutions are recorded, information is gathered that is relevant to revision. Sometimes revisions will be at the level of fine tuning, sometimes they may be more fundamental.

After individual responses are rated and ogive rules have been applied to produce a TPR score, evaluation of the interrelationships among responses is possible. (See chapter 5, this volume, for a description of the methods used to evaluate an item's effectiveness.) Checking for intercorrelations among items and using microvalidation studies, evaluating the spread of ego levels elicited by the item, and finally considering the content represented are useful in evaluating a translated WUSCT (Lasker, 1978; Westenberg et al., 1998).

Nonresponse.   Raters are advised to observe the standard ground rules—rate every response and use the Conformist rating, as a default score for ambiguous or missing responses. Consistent nonresponse should be noted. If a majority of respondents do not complete a stem that has been regularly completed in U.S. samples, it may be an indication of a cultural difference. In U.S. samples, missing responses have been found to be spread across items and have been associated with lower ego level protocols, especially Self-Protective ones. This pattern held true for Ravinder's (1986) Indian and Australian college-aged subjects and Hy's (1986) U.S. sample of Vietnamese refugees. The studies reviewed in this chapter have produced more variety in missing responses. Snarey and Blasi (1980) reported that subjects of higher ego level omitted responses to items referring to family. Kusatsu (1977, 1978) also noted systematic differences in omissions. Items requiring a comment about the self ("I am" and "what troubles me") were more often the ones to be omitted.

In contrast to Ravinder (1986), who reported low omission rates in her Indian college female sample (comparable to the low, relatively random omission patterns found in U.S. samples), Dhruvaragan (1978) reported high rates of missing responses produced by lower SES, rural Indian women. Women of both Vokkaglia and Brahmin castes regularly omitted items referring to the self. Of the sample, 72% chose not to complete the stem "I am." This calls for a rethinking of using the default rule for this item in this setting. The automatic application of E4 as the default score is probably inappropriate, especially since in this sample most TPRs were E2 and E3. Lack of response to "I am" is a result in itself. It does not reveal ego level, but suggests something about the meaning of the self in this context. Setting aside this stem seems reasonable in making a WUSCT rating. At the same time, a 72% omission rate is a meaningful finding and should not be ignored in the broader discussion of the application of the WUSCT method to this context. Sometimes "no response" conveys meaning.

Manual Construction. Researchers who have collected adequately large and representative samples have been able to empirically evaluate item adaptations and develop same-language scoring manuals. Beyond the practical advantages of a manual based on the responses produced in a particular setting, there is the added benefit of being able to employ raters who are matched to respondents in language and culture. In addition, the process of manual construction can be of considerable theoretical value. Creating a culture-specific manual offers a check on the adequacy of prior descriptions of ego levels. The WUSCT was designed to categorize surface manifestations of the underlying course of ego development. Manual construction in a variety of settings may be one of the best methods of determining how common that underlying course of development truly is. The study by Westenberg et al. (1998) is a prime example. By studying a large and representative sample of children and adolescents they discovered that some response categories emerged at different age levels. These anomalies eventually resulted in a revision of the earliest ego levels, at least when referring to ego development in children and adolescents.

THOUGHTS ON FUTURE STUDIES
OF CROSS-CULTURAL DIFFERENCES
IN EGO DEVELOPMENT

Insights From Other Cross-Cultural Studies of Psychological Constructs. The study of ego development in different settings can be informed by literatures on cross-cultural research within psychology. Especially relevant is the cross-cultural application of Kohlberg's method of measuring moral development. Snarey (1985) reviewed 45 studies in which Kohlberg's moral judgment instrument was translated into other languages and adapted to other settings. Moral reasoning was found to be highly associated with middle-class status and experience in complex, urban societies, a finding paralleling the relationship between ego level and SES documented in cross-cultural work with the WUSCT.

Cole (1996), who conducted his own cross-cultural research over three decades, provided an overview on cross-cultural research. He reported that despite some missteps in early efforts to export Western methods of psychological assessment, culture is gaining place in the contemporary zeitgeist. He cited as evidence, developmental psychologists' adoption of an "individual in context as the unit of analysis" perspective (Segall et al., 1990, p. 344, cited in Cole, 1996).

Adult personality methods currently are being tested in international settings. McCrae and Costa (1997) recently reported on a cross-cultural test of their five-factor model of personality traits. Their sample included 7,134 subjects, friends and relatives of psychology students in universities with about 60% of the respondents being students. Subjects represented a wide age range and a variety of education and socioeconomic levels, drawn from seven societies. Factor analysis revealed considerable similarity in factor structures in the different settings, based on "more or less literal translation of items" selected in U.S. samples. The authors noted that although further item analysis might still be useful in refining the translated scales, the results strongly suggest that personality trait structure is universal.

A somewhat less optimistic view about the generalizability of psychological measurement has been expressed by Hall (1997) in a review of the inclusion of minority participation in psychology research conducted in the United States. She described a literature that consistently underrepresents U.S. subcultures. In addition, she noted that when minorities have been included in samples, research designs often did not include an adequate integration of relevant socioeconomic variables with minority status. She concluded that in a nation projected to have by 2050, a 50% population of people of color (a proxy for cultural difference) psychological research may become a less valuable professional resource unless samples are constructed more broadly and more adequate designs address the complexity of culture, ethnicity, and socioeconomic variables.

Improving the Quality of Cross-Cultural Research Methods. Representative sampling and the collection of demographic data such as education level and economic resources are useful given the consistency with which these variables are found to be associated with ego level.

Attention to language issues in implementing the WUSCT method can ensure the quality of ego level estimation and reveal areas of culture-specific difference. Including translation details, such as advice sought on the translation process, results of pilot studies, and background information related to linguistic and sociolinguistic characteristics of the language, informs readers about the setting in which the research takes place.

Procedural problems can be indicators of cultural differences. Sometimes these are results worthy of reporting. Examples include standard item stems that do not discriminate in the new context, item score patterns that vary widely from previous studies, absence of expected correlations between WUSCT scores and measures of SES, and unusual rates of missing data.

The content and methods of other disciplines can improve the quality of ego development studies in new settings. Linguists familiar with the language can address translation issues, and anthropologists offer ethnographic techniques. Economic, political, and religious historians provide a background against which to understand the psychological functions our studies attempt to document. Sociologists map current social structures that are often reflected in item responses and in styles of responding. Such contextual detail can help explain results and provide readers with a base from which to evaluate findings.

ACKNOWLEDGMENTS

We wish to thank Augusto Blasi, Nobomoto Tajima, and Lê Xuân Hy for their comments on this chapter.

Chapter 9
The Place of the WUSCT
for Ego Development in Personality
Measurement

Jane Loevinger
Washington University

The sentence stems that the SCT comprises are not distinctively different from those of other sentence completion tests, which aim to measure other aspects of personality, most often some aspect of adjustment. In consequence, the scoring system for SCTs for one purpose can be applied to other SCTs constructed for other, different purposes. Paradoxically, many of the responses that other SCTs call signs of poor adjustment would be scored by the WUSCT as signs of high ego level.

THE SCORING MANUAL

Although the sentence stems are similar in various SCTs, the scoring manuals are radically different.

The format of the present manual in its first (1970) edition was probably unique, with its categories at each scored level, for each item (sentence stem). All responses used as examples are ones that some person gave. There are no invented or hypothetical responses constructed to fulfill or illustrate a logical definition of that level. Also unique is the graded set of practice exercises, so that novice raters, often graduate students, can acquire some expertise, first with scoring each of the items, then with scoring total protocols, before scoring their own data. At present there are some translations and adaptations of this manual being worked on, so that these features are presumably no longer unique to this manual.

Methodology

Scoring Algorithm. The ogive rules for arriving at a total protocol rating (TPR) constitute a unique algorithm. In fact, very few tests of any sort have a scoring algorithm chosen rationally after considering different possible ones.

Perhaps the pre-eminent claim of the WUSCT is that the concept of what it measures and the method of measurement evolved together. The intertwining of concept formation and measurement technique is frequent in other sciences, but not in psychology. The key element, or device, in this process has been *microvalidation.*

Microvalidation refers to the fact that during the long process of constructing the present scoring manual, a tentative manual was first agreed on, then applied to new data, which had not been used to select the original examples. Then the starting manual, based on intuition and embodying much guesswork, was evaluated, category by category. The use of categories of response is central to this process. To verify and correct intuitive guesswork requires data, that is, replication. Verbatim repetition of all but the simplest responses is rare. Grouping responses into categories gives the equivalent of replication, because all responses within a single category are considered as equivalent, thus permitting revision of the manual on the basis of the new data. The aim of each cycle of this process is not to evaluate the test or the concept as a whole, but to evaluate category by category. The cycle is then repeated with the improved scoring manual and a new sample.

As a result, each scored level is fleshed out with the responses of the (cumulative) sample's subjects. That takes place for each item separately.

After that process has gone on long enough, over enough samples, and with sufficiently variable samples, it will tend to converge, that is, to require few and only trivial changes after each cycle. We then look at all the responses to the several stems together, level by level.

At that point, the manual yields a picture of the persons at each level, in coherent narrative, in their own words, "their own voice" rather than in some abstract, textbook terms.

Thus, description of each level of our variable, ego development, was shaped by responses of our subjects, ultimately totaling thousands of people, drawn widely from the social spectrum, even though no single sample was very large or representative of the population as a whole.

There is, of course, some inference in drawing any conclusions about the persons at each level, beyond the way that they answer sentence completion tests. This inference is bolstered by the knowledge of the way they talk or, usually, write about a wide variety of topics that touch on aspects of everyday life. The revision of the scoring manual continued the process, but required no change in description of the stages.

The SCT As a Window on Personality Structure

The SCT is one of several stage–type theories, of which the best known is Kohlberg's moral judgment interview (Colby & Kohlberg (1987). Kohlberg's scale of developmental stages for moral judgment is recognizably about the same human species as the scale of ego development. The stages of the two conceptions can be set in approximate correspondence, although they concern somewhat different topics or aspects of personality (Blasi, 1998; Loevinger, 1976).

In contrast to the similarity of the stages, the scoring manual for Kohlberg's moral judgment interview is constructed on entirely different lines from this manual. That fact reflects the different philosophical presuppositions, underlying the methods and scoring rules (as explained by Blasi, 1998).

THE FACTOR-TRAIT STRUCTURE
OF PERSONALITY

Contrasting with the various developmental stage descriptions of personality, there is a radically different paradigm for describing the fundamental structure of personality, the factor- trait structure.

The so-called "Big Five" personality trait structure has many adherents, although it is not accepted as universally as its proponents claim.

The central claim of proponents of the Big Five factor-traits is that all of personality can be described in terms of their five factor-derived traits, called (with some variation), extraversion, agreeableness, emotional stability (or neuroticism), conscientiousness, and a fifth factor variously called intellect or openness to experience.

No one has claimed that ego development is the whole of personality structure or the only aspect of personality of any significance. Proponents of the five-factor theory do claim that everything of significance about personality can be encompassed in or described in terms of the five-factor trait structure.

In principle, the stage–type theories and the factor-trait structure theories are compatible and complementary alternative ways of describing the manifold complexities of personality.

At one point, however, just where they seem to be most closely convergent, they are incompatible. The overlapping term is *conscientiousness.*

Inspection of the content of their items shows that for the five-factor theorists conscientiousness and conformity are conflated. Whether measured by rating scales of self or others, or by a checklist of self-report objective test items, or adjective checklists, conscientiousness and conformity are part of a single factor-trait.

However, in the conception of ego development, the contrast between the Conformist stage and the Conscientious stage is at the very heart of the theory. To conflate them is not only to cut the heart out of the theory of ego development, but also to preclude the possibility of ever broadening scope to recognize it or similar stage–type theories, because a similar contrast is at the heart of other stage–type theories, such as Kohlberg's, although not in exactly the same words.

Relations Between the Factor-Traits and the SCT

McCrae and Costa (1980) correlated the SCT with their NEO test for a large sample of adults. They found a correlation with the SCT only for their fifth factor-trait, which they called Openness to Experience.

Westenberg and Block (1993) investigated the relation between the two approaches to personality, factor-trait and developmental stage, more theoretically and in more detail. They point out that each of the Big Five traits is itself an amalgam of several more specific traits. In fact, Costa and McCrae identify six aspects to each.

If two aspects of one NEO factor are heterogeneous with respect to relation with ego development, the relation between the NEO trait and the SCT will be attenuated. For example, neuroticism, as conceptualized by Costa and McCrae, contains several subdomains such as impulsivity, hostility, depression, and anxiety.

Some of these subdomains, including impulsivity and hostility, are expected to be related to ego development, whereas others, including depression and anxiety, are less clearly developmental, or possibly not at all.

Another possible complication is that the sample on which a study is being done may not vary with respect to the stages and traits at issue. For example, the trait of impulsivity is very different at the Impulsive stage than at the Self-Protective or Conformist stages. On the other hand, Conformists probably will not differ at all from Conscientious stage persons on impulsivity. Thus, a sample consisting of Conformists and Conscientious stage persons will make it look like there is no relation between Impulsivity and ego level.

There are now many personality tests that offer not only computerized scoring but also computer programs for interpreting the test scores and writing reports of them.

Only after mastering and using the scoring manual will the student or researcher realize that he or she has acquired much more than a psychometric method, indeed, an insight into a dynamic dimension of character and personality, implicitly encoded in the scoring manual.

That gain in insight helps establish the unique place of the WU SCT contrasting with the many computer-scorable tests of personality.

Chapter 10
A New Version of the WUSCT: The Sentence Completion Test for Children and Youths (SCT-Y)

P. Michiel Westenberg
Philip D. A. Treffers
Martine J. Drewes
Leiden University, the Netherlands

Form 81 of the Washington University Sentence Completion Test (WUSCT) was developed for adult men and women, but is assumed to be adequate also for adolescent boys and girls. It is unknown, however, to what extent Form 81 can be extended downwards, both in terms of the item content and in terms of the scoring manual. Would Form 81 and the scoring manual still be appropriate at age 16 … 14 … 12 … 10 … 8 …?

Loevinger and colleagues developed a seperate version of the WUSCT specifically for boys and girls, Form 2-77 (see Appendix C, this volume), but age recommendations or restrictions are not offered. At what age should one switch from Form 81 to Form 2-77, and what is the minimum age at which Form 2-77 can be used? Moreover, are scoring manuals derived from predominantly adult responses adequate for the scoring of SCT protocols from children and youths? And consequently, are stage descriptions based on adult responses representative for children and youths? And if one decides to use Form 2-77, how should responses be rated to those items for which the present manual does not provide scoring manuals?

In response to these questions, a new SCT form plus scoring manual, the SCT-Y, was developed for measuring ego development in children and youths.

A STUDY OF EGO DEVELOPMENT IN YOUTH

A new SCT for children and youths (SCT-Y), including a complete set of scoring manuals, was developed in the context of studying the clinical implications of ego development. The research was carried out at Leiden University's Academic Center for Child and Adolescent Psychiatry *Curium*, the Netherlands. It involved an outpatient population and a representative sample of school children and students. The research was carried out in three phases: a pilot study ($N = 932$), a normative study ($N = 1,841$), and a test–retest study ($N = 178$). A more detailed description of the samples and procedures is given by Westenberg, Jonckheer, Treffers, and Drewes (1998).

The selection of the items for the SCT-Y and the development of a scoring manual proceeded simultaneously. In fact, the development of the scoring manual led to changes in the description of the lowest ego levels, when referring to the development of children and adolescents. Despite the entwining of the construction of the SCT-Y and the construction of the manual, we first discuss the construction of the SCT-Y, and then we provide a brief outline of the manual-making process and the proposed adjustments in the description of the earliest ego levels.

Construction of an SCT for Children and Youths

For consistency with past research on ego development, we relied on the most frequently used SCT forms to select items for the first phase of the project. Form 81 is the current standard of the WUSCT (Loevinger, 1985), and the present revision of the scoring manual covers all of its 36 items (Hy & Loevinger, 1996). Therefore, the initial pool of items included all 36 items of Form 81, in the same order. Form 2-77 provided 8 additional items not included in Form 81, and 7 more items were added to cover new ground (e.g., peer relations and fears). The 51 items were reduced to 32 items on the basis of the following criteria, some of which are identical to the criteria for revising the WUSCT (see chapter 2, this volume).

Criterion 1: Maximum Overlap With Form 81 of the WUSCT. For consistency with past research on ego development and to build on the current revision of the scoring manual (Hy & Loevinger, 1996), the items of Form 81 received the highest priority. If all were equal, an item from Form 81 was chosen over any other item. If necessary, items from Form 81 were adapted to make them more appropriate for young respondents. For example, on the form for boys, the item "When I am with a woman—" was changed to "When I am with a girl—." The results of our study show that the rephrased version draws the same type of responses from boys as the original item draws from men.

Criterion 2: Appropriateness for All Age Cohorts (Ages 8–18). T h e items had to be appropriate for all respondents, irrespective of age, experience, or level of cognitive and sexual maturation. For example, items pertaining to sex do not carry the same meaning for respondents of the different age cohorts: The young children in our study did not know how to respond, adolescents were reluctant to respond, whereas young adults were able to respond from their own experience. Items about sex were therefore deleted, as were two items concerning the rights and obligations of husbands and wives (e.g., "A husband has a right to—").

Criterion 3: Comparable Forms for Boys and Girls. The male and female forms were to consist of identical or gender-equivalent items. For example, the item "If I were king—" (Form 2-77) was replaced by "If I were in charge—," because young girls often did not respond to the item "If I were king—" or they responded that they could not be king. We were not ready to delete this item, however, because it refers to the crucial concept of control. The phrasing "If I were in charge—" appeared to be gender-neutral in terms of the elicited responses.

Criterion 4: Optimal Variety of Item Content. "Ego" represents one's general frame of reference not specific to any content. Therefore, the items need to represent as many different areas as possible, without overloading subjects with too many items. To optimize the variation among a limited number of items, the number of "duplications" was minimized. For example, the item "Women are lucky because—" is used only on the male form, and the item "Men are lucky because—" is used only on the female form, whereas both items are present on the male and female Forms 81 and 2-77. Another way to maximize content variety was to add a few items covering new areas, such as peer relations ("Good friends—") and fears ("My biggest fear—").

Criterion 5: Face Validity (Experienced Relevance). The task of completing sentences has face validity for youngsters. They appreciate the opportunity to express their own thoughts and feelings in their own words. But some of the items, or combinations of items, diminished the experienced validity of the SCT. The greatest threat to face validity was an overrepresentation of gender-specific items. Many young respondents rebelled against the repeated suggestion that men and women are different in so many ways, and in the end this rebellion was turned against the SCT itself. Therefore, the proportion of such items was lowered to a tolerable level. For example, "A woman/man should always—" was deleted, and the number of duplications was reduced (see Criterion 4).

A second detriment to face validity was the use of third-person items. The majority of the respondents, especially the youngest ones, do not appreciate the opportunity to respond from a third-person perspective. Many respondents asked questions about it, expressed doubts about the usefulness of such items, and too often did not respond at all. The resistance against these items calls into question whether subjects respond more truthfully or genuinely to third-person questions. Moreover, third-person items complicate the work of the manual-constructor and the rater; did the subject respond from his or her own or someone else's perspective? Therefore, third-person items were not used or were changed to the first person (e.g., "Sometimes I wished that—" instead of "Sometimes she/he wished that—").

Criterion 6: Item Validity (Item-Total Correlation). The SCT for ego development is assumed to measure a single construct; hence, the items are expected to correlate with the total score. Items with low item-total correlations, in any age cohort, were deleted from the item pool. Most often, low item-total correlations were due to low response variability. For example, "A girl has a right to—" elicited basically the same response, "—*whatever she wants,*" independent of age or ego level. Hence, the item-total correlation for this item was relatively low. This item was removed from the item pool, as were other items with low item validity.

Criterion 7: Adequate Test Length. The effort and motivation required from subjects to complete each item stem has to be weighed against the number of items required for optimal test reliability (i.e., homogeneity of the item scores, interrater agreement on total protocol ratings [TPRs], and the test–retest stability of the total score). Thirty-two items yield reliable scores while they appear to require the right amount of time and effort; not too long and not too brief. A practical advantage is that 32 items fit on two pages, while still allowing the youngest and the oldest subjects sufficient room to write their responses. The number of 32 corresponds to a previous version of Form 2-77.

Criterion 8: Equivalent Meaning in Dutch. This criterion was due to our research circumstances; the research had to be carried out with Dutch subjects, and the items had to be translated. Equivalence between Dutch and U.S. versions of the items was achieved through a careful process of translation, back-translation, try-outs, modifications, and so on (see Appendix F, this volume, for a discussion of translating item stems). Only a few items in the initial item pool did not have a clear equivalent in Dutch. For example, the Dutch equivalent of "A man's job—" did not convey the same meaning, and was deleted from the item pool. In some cases, translation difficulties led to an improved version of the item. For example, the concept "Raising a family—" does not have a straightforward equivalent in Dutch, but the alternative version "Raising children—" worked very well with young children. In other cases, translatability was influenced by age. For example, the item "When a child will not join in group activities—" is suitable for U.S. children as young as 8 years of age; hence, the item can be used in all age cohorts. In Dutch, however, the literal translation of "will not join in group activities" did not sound sufficiently familiar to young children, and was slightly adjusted to "will not do things in a group." A blind back-translation of the latter, however, came very close to the American original "will not join in group activities." It was therefore concluded that the U.S. original and the adjusted Dutch version are equivalent, both in terms of the meaning of the item and in terms of the elicited responses.

THE SCT-Y

The final set of 32 items consists of clear equivalents in English and in Dutch, appropriate for 8-to 18-year-old respondents, with separate forms for girls and boys. The English version of the SCT-Y is presented in Table 10.1 (the actual test protocols, in English or in Dutch, may be obtained from the authors). The SCT-Y

TABLE 10.1

Comparison of the SCT-Y With Forms 81 and 2-77 of theWUSCT

SCT-Y (Girls/Boys)	WUSCT Form 81 (Women/Men)	WUSCT Form 2-77 (Girls/Boys)
1. When a child will not join in group activities	1. Same	3. Same
2. Raising children	2. Raising a family	20. Raising a family
3. When I am criticized	3. Same	30. Same
4. If I were in charge		31. If I were king
5. Being with other people	5. Same	6. Same
6. The thing I like about myself is	6. Same	5. Same
7. My mother and I	7. Same	4. My mother/father and I
8. What gets me into trouble is	8. Same	9. Same
9. Education	9. Same	8. Same
10.When people are helpless	10. Same	32. Same
11.When I am afraid		
12.A good father	12. Same	10. Same [girls]
13.My biggest fear		
14.I feel sorry	16. Same	11. Same
15.When they avoided me		19. Same
16.Rules are	18. Same	16. Same
17.Crime and delinquency could be halted if	19. Same	28. Same
18.Men/Women are lucky because	20/11. Same	34/13. Same
19. I just can't stand people who	21. Same	23. Same
20.At times I worry about	22. At times she/he worried about	14. At times she/he worried about
21.I am	23. Same	21. Same
22.A girl/boy feels good when	24/17. A woman/man feels good when	26. Same
23.My main problem is	25. Same	27. Same
24.Good friends		
25.The worst thing about being a woman/man	27. Same	12. Same
26. A good mother	28. Same	10. Same [boys]
27. When I am with a boy/girl	29. When I am with a man/woman	
28. Sometimes I wished that	30. Sometimes she/he wished that	29. Sometimes she/he wished that
29. My father	31. Same	24. Same
30. If I can't get what I want	32. Same	25. Same
31. My conscience bothers me if	35. Same	35. Same
32. I felt proud that I		15. She/He felt proud that she/he

(continued)

TABLE 10.1
(continued)

SCT-Y (Girls/Boys)	WUSCT Form 81 (Women/Men)	WUSCT Form 2-77 (Girls/Boys)
	4. A man's job	2. A man's job [boys]
	13. A girl has a right to	22. A girl has a right to [girls]
	15. A wife should	2. A wife should [girls]
	26. A husband has a right to	22. A husband has a right to [boys]
	36. A woman/man should always	36. A woman/man should always
	14. When they talked about sex, I	
	33. Usually she/he felt that sex	
	34. For a woman a career is	
		1. If I had more money
		7. If my mother
		17. When she/he thought of her/his mother, she/he
		18. When I get mad
		33. When my mother spanked me, I

Note. The actual test protocols of the SCT-Y, in English or in Dutch, may be obtained from the authors (e-mail: p.m.westenberg@thuisnet.leidenuniv.nl). A U.S. version of the Dutch scoring manual for the SCT-Y is in preparation. Meanwhile, the SCT-Y may be scored by bilingual raters using the Dutch manual. The test protocols of Forms 81 and 2-77 of the WUSCT are provided in Appendix C.

represents a cross-section of the WUSCT Form 81 and Form 2-77: Twenty-two items are identical to the items of either form, 7 items are adjusted versions of the items of either form, and only 3 items were completely new (for a comparison, see Table 10.1).

The youngest children (8-year-olds) respond well to the current set of items, provided that their reading and writing skills are sufficiently developed. All respondents, regardless of age, are instructed to seek the assistance of the test administrator in case of questions or comments. For example, if a child cannot read the word *delinquency,* the test administrator may read the word out loud. Reading a word out loud usually suffices. If the subject does not know a particular word or concept, the test administrator is instructed to give a standard explanation. For example, delinquency is explained in terms of "doing bad things, misdeeds." The administrator is allowed to explain any word or concept, as long as they refrain from giving or suggesting any completions. It is our experience that only the youngest children need assistance, and that it does not impede the proces of completing the items.

A Scoring Manual for the SCT-Y

Form 81 of the WUSCT (Loevinger, 1985) was the jumping-off point for developing the SCT-Y, and the revised scoring manual for Form 81 (Hy & Loevinger, 1996) was the starting point for developing a scoring manual for the SCT-Y. Twenty-six

SCT-Y items stem from Form 81, allowing child and adolescent responses to these items to be categorized with the revised item manuals, at least as a first step. Three SCT-Y items stem from Form 2-77, allowing them to be scored with additional but unrevised item manuals (Loevinger et al., 1970; Redmore et al., 1978). For the 3 new items, new scoring manuals had to be made. To construct and evaluate a scoring manual for the SCT-Y, we closely followed the procedures used by Loevinger and her colleagues in developing and revising the scoring manual for the WUSCT (see chapters 1, 2, 6, this volume).

The revised manual for Form 81 of the WUSCT (Hy & Loevinger, 1996) was based primarily on responses from (young) adults and contains no responses from children and relatively few responses from adolescents (see chapter 3, this volume). Therefore, the adequacy of the revised scoring manual for rating child and adolescent responses may be questioned: Are child and adolescent responses at all represented in a scoring manual based on adult responses, and if so, are similar response categories characteristic of the same ego levels in children and youths versus those of adults?

The data gave a positive answer to the first part of the question: About 80% of the child and adolescent responses to the 26 common items could be classified on the basis of the revised scoring manual. The similar responses resulted in content-equivalent response categories in the scoring manual for children and youths. The data gave a negative answer to the second part of the question, however: Only about 50% of the content-equivalent response categories was characteristic of the same ego level in children and youths, whereas the other half of the similar response categories was not characteristic of the same ego level in children and youths. The latter set of response categories was mostly characteristic of lower ego levels in children and youths. This "downshift" of response categories was particularly striking at the lowest three ego levels; many Conformist and Self-Protective response categories "dropped" one or two levels, whereas relatively few Self-Aware or Conscientious categories dropped to lower levels. For example, following Loevinger's microvalidation procedure (see chapter 1, this volume), the response category "When I am criticized—*I get mad, angry,*" placed at the Self-Protective level in the revised scoring manual (Hy & Loevinger, 1996), was most prevalent at the Impulsive level in the sample of children and adolescents. This inconsistency at the level of the manual, however, appears to be consistent with Loevinger's description of the Impulsive level.

Other downshifts, however, appeared inconsistent with Loevinger's descriptions. For example, the response category "When people are helpless— *I help them,*" placed at the Conformist level in the revised manual (Hy & Loevinger, 1996), was most typical of Impulsive youngsters. This downshift appeared inconsistent with Loevinger's descriptions of the Impulsive as well as the Conformist level, and contributed to accommodations in the description of both levels.

In summary, due to the downshift of content-equivalent categories and the addition of the newly constructed response categories, the completed scoring manual for the SCT-Y offers a somewhat revised picture of the Impulsive, Self-Protective and Conformist levels, which were still generally in keeping with Loevinger's theoretical description.

Revised Description of the First Three Ego Levels

In the following synopsis, the differences between the two data sets receive more attention than the similarities (for an elaborate discussion of the similarities and differences, see Westenberg et al., 1998).

Impulsive Level. Similar to the current description of the Impulsive level based on responses from (young) adults, responses from Impulsive children and youths suggest a preoccupation with aggression, a dependent interpersonal style, an emphasis on concrete wishes and interactions, and the presence of basic and extreme emotions. Despite the preoccupation with aggression, however, *blatant* forms of aggression were not typical of Impulsive children and adolescents; aggressive reactions were displayed mainly in response to the frustration of dependency needs. Moreover, impulsivity in young Impulsives is not limited to aggressive impulses. Indeed, empathic impulses were present in 30% to 40% of their protocols (e.g., "When people are helpless— *I help them*"). Another difference is that Impulsive children and adolescents were less oppositional and defiant than their older counterparts and were more open to rules and guidance generally. Impulsive youngsters were characterized more by a sense of vulnerability (e.g., concern about being the victim of aggression), by a dependent coping style (e.g., protection- and assistance-seeking in challenging situations), and by positive interactions (e.g., the desire to do things with others).

Self-Protective Level. Congruent with the present description of the Self-Protective level, responses from Self-Protective youngsters indicate a preoccupation with control, a punitive attitude toward misconduct, an opportunistic sense of morality, and a hedonistic view of life. According to Loevinger's description of the Self-Protective person, control is expressed in a manipulative and exploitative attitude toward others. We found, however, that an outright manipulative and exploitative attitude toward other people is not characteristic of Self-Protective adolescents. The latter were characterized more by self-focused forms of control (e.g., general denial of hurt feelings, disappointments, and problems), by a self-sufficient attitude (e.g., the desire to take care of oneself), by a live-and-let-live philosophy (e.g., all people should be allowed to do their own thing), and by instrumental but appreciative relations (e.g., having good friends and parents is useful).

Conformist Level.   As with the Conformist person described by Loevinger, Conformist youngsters in the present study appeared rule-bound, other-centered, focused on social desirability, and perceptive of global emotions. In addition, they were concerned with helpful attitudes (e.g., they are motivated to alleviate distress in others), equal and reciprocal relations (e.g., good friends get on with each other), and egalitarian values (e.g., dislike of competitiveness and hierarchical relations). Instead of being focused solely on appearances and concrete behaviors in specific situations, feelings appeared key in several respects: it is enjoyable to be with others in its own right, it makes one feel bad to disappoint others, it makes one feel good to help someone in need, it makes one feel bad to do wrong, and so on.

These differences for the earliest ego levels are attributed to the age difference between Loevinger's samples and the samples of the present study. The younger age of our subjects allowed us to study hundreds of low-level subjects going through these stages in due time, whereas the older age of Loevinger's subjects allowed for the study of relatively few low-level subjects who are delayed in their development. The differences may, however, also be due partly to the differences between the Dutch and U.S. culture and language.

To be sure about the correct explanation of the found differences, a similar project would have to be carried out in the United States. Is ego developent in U.S. youngsters comparable to ego development in their Dutch peers? To answer this question and to construct a U.S. scoring manual for the SCT-Y, we are collecting SCT-Y data in the context of various research projects in the United States. The aim is to collect SCT-Y data on a representative sample of U.S. children and youths. Meanwhile, pilot testing in the United States indicates that the SCT-Y can be scored reliably by bilingual raters using the Dutch manual.

CONCLUSION

The findings of our study underscored the need for a separate SCT for children and youths, both in terms of the SCT form and in terms of the scoring manual. At the same time, these findings reaffirm the general utility of the WUSCT as a measure of ego development, even in children, and support the premise that adult ego levels are related to development occurring in childhood and adolescence.

ACKNOWLEDGMENTS

This research was supported by grants from the Dutch National Fund for Mental Health (*Nationaal Fonds Geestelijke Volksgezondheid,* Utrecht) and the Frijling Prins Fund (Amsterdam). We appreciate the assistance of Vicki K. Carlson and Lawrence D. Cohn in finding the best (back-)translation of the items while maintaining suitability for all age cohorts. This chapter greatly benefited from comments by Vicki K. Carlson.

Chapter 11

Other Uses of the WUSCT

Jane Loevinger
Washington University
Lê Xuân Hy
Center for Multicultural Human Services

Although the WUSCT and its scoring manual have been evolved explicitly for the purpose of measuring the complex developmental strand we call *ego development,* the rich vein of thought evoked by the test lends itself to other uses as well.

Rogers (1987, 1998) evolved a scoring manual for judging and comparing orientations toward justice and rights, versus orientation toward care and responsibility, as those orientations are manifest in sentence completions such as those of the WUSCT.

The WUSCT was originally designed for a study of women (see chapter 1, this volume), but it has been broadened to apply to men also (see chapter 2, this volume). Many stems in the SCT are pertinent to attitudes about gender differences, even though the SCT was not designed for that purpose. Such topics are valuable transducers to reveal fundamental attitudes about many things, and those same attitudes are expressive of ego or character development.

The current revision of the SCT scoring manual (see chapter 3, this volume) has been based on more than 1,000 cases drawn widely from the social spectrum in various parts of the United States. To date, the revised SCT has not been applied to large matched samples of men and women; but some attitudes are so widespread throughout the various subsamples that were used in the manual revision that they permit some broad generalizations, which remain to be confirmed by large-scale controlled sampling.

Most of the items are the same on the men's and women's forms of the current version of the test (Form 81). For most items, the answers that men give are within the same range as those given by women, and the same scoring manual is used for both. Items that are not identical are paired, differing only by gender. One of the most differentiating pairs of items asks for the worst thing about being a man (men's form), or the worst thing about being a woman (women's form). Men think that they have all or most of the responsibility, but women also think they have most of the responsibility. There are, of course, unique ways of saying this, although most just say it bluntly. One woman wrote that the worst thing about being a woman "is that you are the default parent."

Because it is now virtually the norm to have both parents working, mothers are usually the ones who stay home from work when their children are sick, or they have responsibility for the children and the housework.

The responsibility most often complained about by men is the need to support a family, but many men say there is no worst thing. Most women have no trouble coming up with some worst thing, such as lower status, fewer opportunities, lower pay for the same work, wearing pantyhose, or fear of pregnancy. The most popular single answer is menstruation. The vernacular name for it a few generations ago was "the curse." That term is no longer current, but evidently the sentiment is unchanged. There is no corresponding physical complaint among men that receives such emphasis.

Concern for appearance is attributed to women by both men and women, but opinions differ on whether it is an asset or a burden. On the one hand, "Women are lucky because they can wear beautiful clothes," but on the other hand, "the worst thing about being a woman is that you always have to be worried about your appearance." It is rare for any answer to mention anything about men's appearance.

Many of the comparisons given here depended on the contrast between the present scoring manual and the first edition, published in 1970.

Chapter 8 reveals further the network of relations of the SCT to other variables, including those found in languages other than English.

Changing attitudes about women's work are reflected in the SCT. "Women are lucky because after they get married, they don't have to work," used to be a popular type of answer (ignoring Ogden Nash's warning, "Safety pins and bassinets await the girl who fascinets"), but is no longer common.

Some women used to say that having a career was acceptable for a woman as long as it is subordinate to her husband's career. That is a rare sentiment today, even among men. The idea that a woman should subordinate her wishes and her time entirely to the welfare of her children and/or her husband is no longer fashionable.

Rebellion against being pressured to conform to social stereotypes is now common among both men and women. Presumably feminist and women's liberation movements began the trend among women.

The once popular injunctions by women to women to always be feminine are now largely replaced by injunctions for women to be themselves. In fact, responses to "A woman should always—," a stem found only on the women's form, are remarkably similar to responses to "A man should always—," found on the men's form.

Many men object to the fact that they have to act "macho" to gain respect of other men.

NEUROPSYCHOLOGICAL SCREENING

Along an entirely different line than the use of the SCT for surveying gender attitudes, Hy (unpublished manuscript) suggests that the SCT is suitable for screening individuals for brain damage. Loss of the ability to write clear, logical language can be a sign of brain damage. Hy pointed out that many of the more specific signs of neuropsychological impairment are the same as signs of low ego level. The overlap is so great that adding the WUSCT to a routine battery for clinical assessment can increase its usefulness as at least a screening for neuropsychological damage. By the same token, however, some suspected cases of low ego level may prove to be cases of brain damage.

Some of the same signs may be caused by insufficient familiarity with the English language. However, an alert examiner can usually ascertain by other signs or by direct questioning whether unfamiliarity with the language causes the low score.

Ways of distinguishing low ego level from neuropsychological impairment remain to be discovered in future research.

Appendix A
The Family Problems Scale as a Measure of Authoritarian Family Ideology

Jane Loevinger
Washington University
Kitty LaPerriere
Ackerman Institute for the Family, New York
Claire Ernhart
Metro Health Medical Center, Cleveland, Ohio

The rationale of the Family Problems scale (FPS) is given briefly in chapter 1, and more extensively in (Loevinger, Sweet, Ossorio, & LaPerriere, 1962). Scoring keys were derived by homogeneous keying.

The closest to confirmation of any of the Freudian psychosexual stages was a cluster of items measuring Orderliness.

Another cluster of items seemed to be a combination of conventionality and anxiety. Another cluster signified rejection of women's biological role. It was positively correlated with conventionality–anxiety, which included a rigidly conventional adherence to woman's social role. Thus, no single cluster measured acceptance of or adherence to the "feminine role," a popular concept of that time. The largest and most interesting cluster appeared to measure Authoritarian Family Ideology (AFI).

Ernhart, in order to investigate the concept of AFI, formed a new sample of 1,589 young women drawn widely from the social spectrum, including a broader racial mix of subjects than the original homogeneous keying sample (Loevinger et al., 1962). In Ernhart's new sample, 934 cases answered every single item on the form of the FPS used. Those protocols were then subjected to a new homogeneous keying analysis, exactly as in the previous study (Loevinger et al., 1962). An additional group of 104 cases was used to cross-validate the new homogeneous keys.

As in the 1962 study, the largest cluster of items was that measuring AFI, with many items the same and the content clearly recognizable as the same as the original measure of AFI. As in 1962, there were several smaller clusters, to which psychologically plausible titles could be attached, but they did not reproduce any of the smaller clusters of the 1962 study. Moreover, AFI had more items and more obvious diversity of content, and at the same time a higher K-R 20 (coefficient alpha; Ernhart & Loevinger, 1969). There were 104 additional cases usable to cross-validate the homogeneous keying. Of the remaining tested cases, 432 were suitable to use for an analysis of variance (anova) of the scoring keys just obtained.

The independent variables of the anova were race (Black, White) education (grade school, part high school, finished high school, part college) and parity (up to four children). Many of the women were tested postpartum. Age was confounded with education and parity and controlled through covariance analysis. As before, AFI was correlated significantly with education, age, and parity, presumably representing experience in childrearing. Contrary to popular belief and to the belief of some professionals, middle-class mothers were more permissive in childrearing than were women of lesser education.

The novel aspect of Ernhart's research was to look at the homogeneity of the scoring keys within and between the demographic subgroups. AFI proved to be a robust cluster by every criterion, within or between demographic subgroups. By contrast, none of the smaller clusters was homogeneous within demographic subgroups. This result throws into question whether factor analysis is the royal road to determining the trait structure of personality. In Ernhart's data, not only did different demographic groups have different mean scores and standard deviations, the interrelations of the items and subtests were different; hence the structure of traits was presumably different. Although the factorial method she used was homogeneous keying (Loevinger, Gleser, & DuBois, 1953), the reasoning applies as well to other more orthodox factorial methods.

By every criterion, AFI is a robust trait. In view of the potential importance of AFI, and its robustness, it appears worthy of further study. Therefore Ernhart abbreviated the 110-item FPS to "Raising Children," having only 40 items, and changing the title to the questionnaire to avoid the term problem, which may put off some subjects.

Scoring Key for AFI, for the Questionnaire, "Raising Children":

The following items are scored plus one if the A alternative is checked: 1; 3; 5; 10; 12; 15; 15; 17; 21; 22 ; 24; 26; 27; 29; 31; 33; 34; ; 35; 36.
All other items are scored plos one if the B alternative is checked.
No norms are available, but these scores can be correlated with other variables.

RAISING CHILDREN

Name... Date................

Home address....................................... Age.................

Education: Circle highest grade completed: 1 2 3 4 5 6 7 8
            (High School) 9 10 11 12
            (College) Freshman Sophomore Junior Senior

Show by mark (X) graduation or successful completion of:
            Elementary school.....   Junior high school.....
            Senior high school....   College.....   Other............

Marital Status: Single... Married... Widowed... Divorced or separated...

How many children do you have?.....   Age of oldest child.........

What is the family religion........................

Instructions:

        This booklet contains opinions which some people have about
parents and children. You will notice that there are two opinions about the
same thing with the same number in front of them. Put a check mark in front
of the one you agree with. Mark one opinion of each pair.

        Sometimes you will find that you don't agree with either one.
Then choose the one that is closer to your own idea, or the one that is a
little better. If you agree with both, choose the one you like better.

        Work quickly and do not linger over any one item. Check one
opinion of each pair.

Examples:

X...A. Most married couples want to have at least one child.
....B. Many married couples don't ever want to have children.

....A ' When a new-born baby cried, his mother can always quiet him quickly.
X...B   When a new-born baby cries, his mother sometimes does not know what
        to do for him.

Notice that sentence A is marked in the first example and sentence B in the
second example. Now go ahead with the others. Choose one of each pair.

1...A. You can spoil a tiny baby by picking him up every time he cries.
....B. You cannot spoil a tiny baby by picking him up every time he cries.

2...A. Parents should not pay any attention when small children use naughty words.
....B. Parents should punish small children when they use naughty words.

3...A. A father should be his son's best pal.
....B. A father should not try to be his son's best pal.

4...A. Overalls are often the most practical thing for a little girl to wear.
....B. A little girl should wear dresses instead of overalls.

5...A. If a mother trains her baby properly, he will not need diapers after he is one year old.
....B. It is better not to start toilet training a baby until he is at least a year old.

6...A. Teen-agers cannot be expected to be grateful to their parents.
....B. After all the sacrifices parents make, teen-age children should be grateful to them.

7...A. It is more fun to watch a child play than to watch him eat well.
....B. It is more fun to watch a child eat well than to watch him play.

8...A. If a young mother finds her baby puzzling, she should talk to some older, more experienced woman about her problems.
....B. If a young mother finds her baby puzzling, she should talk to friends her own age who have the same kinds of problems.

9...A. Small babies should be fed when they are hungry.
....B. Small babies should be fed on a regular schedule.

10...A. A three-year-old who wets his pants should be made to feel ashamed of himself.
.....B. There is no use making a child feel ashamed when he wets his pants.

11...A. A child of 8 should have a little money to spend without telling his parents.
.....B. A child of 8 should tell his parents how he spends his money.

12...A. The best kind of family life is the kind where the whole family does everything together.
.....B. Everyone, even a child, needs some privacy in his life.

13...A. A three-year-old is likely to be more disturbed by having his tonsils out than a six-year-old.
.....B. It is better to have tonsils taken out at three than at six, since a three-year-old soon forgets.

14...A. A house that looks a little untidy is more attractive than one where everything is always picked up.
.....B. An attractive house has a place for everything and everything in its place.

15...A.   It is up to the parents to train a child to have regular toilet
           habits.
.....B.   If too much fuss isn't made, a child's toilet training will take
           care of itself.

16...A.   If a boy of 6 or 7 lies or steals, he should be punished severely.
.....B.   Lying and stealing aren't very serious in boys 6 or 7.

17...A.   No child should be permitted to strike his mother.
.....B.   A mother should not be harsh with a small child who strikes her.

18...A.   Mothers should prepare good meals and let children eat what they like.
.....B.   Mothers should teach children to eat everything on their plates.

19...A.   Parents should not ask about a five-year-old's bowel movement unless
           he is sick.
.....B.   A child of five should be reminded every day to have his bowel
           movement.

20...A.   More people are doing a good job of raising children today than 30
           years ago.
.....B.   Fewer people are doing a good job of raising children today than
           30 years ago.

21...A.   If a little girl is a tomboy, her mother should try to get her
           interested in dolls and playing house.
.....B.   If a little girl is a tomboy, her mother should let her play boys'
           games.

22...A.   It is important to see that a young child does not form bad habits.
.....B.   If a young child is happy, he will not form bad habits.

23...A.   If a three-year-old still sucks his thumb, his mother should prevent
           it or punish him.
.....B.   A mother should not prevent a three-year-old from sucking his thumb
           or punish him for doing so.

24...A.   If parents taught their children obedience, the children wouldn't
           get into trouble with the law.
.....B.   When a child gets into trouble with the law, it is usually because
           his parents don't love him enough.

25...A.   Children should be allowed to criticize their parents.
.....B.   Children should not be disrespectful of their parents.

26...A.   If an older child strikes a younger one, he should always be punished.
.....B.   If an older child strikes a younger one, he may have a good reason for
           it.

27...A.   Boys like to date "fast" girls, but when it comes to getting married,
           they choose girls for whom they have more respect.
.....B.   Most boys marry the same kind of girl they have been going out with.

28...A.   A four-year-old is more interested in sex differences than an eight-year-old.

.....B.   An eight-year-old is more interested in sex differences than a four-year-old.

29...A.   Punishing a child doesn't do any good if you make up to him right afterwards.

.....B.   It is best to make up with a child right after punishing him.

30...A.   It is foolish for a woman to spend time cleaning house when she has a bad cold.

.....B.   A woman should keep her house neat even when she has a bad cold.

31...A.   Most children nowadays aren't taught to respect their parents enough.

.....B.   Children have as much respect for their parents nowadays as they ever did.

32...A.   It is fun to hear a five-year-old tell big stories.

.....B.   A five-year-old should be taught not to tell big stories that aren't true.

33...A.   Most mothers nowadays let their children get away with too much.

.....B.   Most mothers nowadays do a pretty good job of raising their children.

34...A.   In the long run, how much you achieve is what gives you satisfaction.

.....B.   In the long run it's not where you get but how much fun you have getting there that counts.

35...A.   It is best for small children not to watch their parents get dressed and undressed.

.....B.   It is all right for small children to watch their parents get dressed and undressed.

36...A.   Once you've made rules for your children, you should never go back on them.

.....B.   In family living it is often best not to be too strict about rules.

37...A.   It is silly for a woman to worry about coming home alone at night.

.....B.   A woman should never be alone on the streets at night.

38...A.   It is all right to tell a lie to save a friend.

.....B.   It is not right to lie, even if someone will be hurt by the truth.

39...A.   It is more important to have pretty things in a house than to keep it spotless.

.....B.   It is more important to have the house spotless than to have pictures and flowers in it.

40...A.   If a wife doesn't like housework, she should let some of it go and do things she likes better.

.....B.   There is no excuse for a wife not keeping up with her housework.

Appendix B

Notes on WUSCT Rating Practice
Exercises (Provided in Appendices A and B
of Hy & Loevinger, 1996)

Jane Loevinger
Washington University

with assistance of
Vicki Carlson
Washington University
Lê Xuân Hy
Center for Multicultural Human Services

ITEM EXERCISES

The examples are meant to lead new raters into every part of the item manual and to show some characteristic responses for various E levels that apply to other items also. Examples that appear verbatim in the item manual were avoided, although a few may appear verbatim in category titles. Unusually difficult examples were usually avoided. The exercise is not meant to be a hard test but rather an easy introduction. Very long responses are avoided in item exercises because they usually express unique concerns of the person giving the response, whereas item exercises should introduce raters to the kinds of responses they are likely to see from their own subjects. Rating the item exercises is often more time-consuming than rating for a large sample, for which the rater will ordinarily be given an item response list for each item. When all the answers to a single item are rated at once, the rating goes quickly, because there are many easy and obvious responses that are verbatim in the manual, and the other responses are often so similar that one does not have to begin all over again to find where each one belongs.

PROTOCOL EXERCISES

The purpose of the protocol exercises is first of all to illustrate how the total protocol rating (TPR) is arrived at using the ogive rules and also using the item sum. The protocols chosen are all ones from real people, so inevitably have some responses that are difficult to rate. They have been chosen to illustrate the variety that can be found in real work. They come from both men and women, they come from various parts of the country (mostly from the United States but perhaps a few from Canada), from various social classes, various educational levels, various ages, and various E levels. They were collected by various investigators in connection with different projects. We are aware that age, educational level, and intelligence will affect responses, but these exercises show how TPR is obtained without direct reference to those confounded variables. Some high-level protocols are longer than average, and some low-level protocols have many misspellings, but those are not admissible considerations in rating. The rater should try to guess what the subject meant to say, and rate that. In order to keep the rater focussed on the rating task rather than on confounded variables, in some places we have corrected spelling or interpolated our guess as to what was meant. Raters should be warned that real protocols from all social and educational classes will reflect the decline of literacy today, but that is not being rated here.

The item-sum TPR parameters (see Table 4.1) were set to approximate as closely as possible the ogive TPRs. In the practice exercises, that is the case.

Appendix C

Current Version of the WUSCT(Form 81 for Women and Men) and Previously Used Forms for Adults and Children

SENTENCE COMPLETION FOR WOMEN (Form 81)

Name_____Age____Marital Status____Education_____

Instructions: Complete the following sentences.

1. When a child will not join in group activities

2. Raising a family

3. When I am criticized

4. A man's job

5. Being with other people

6. The thing I like about myself is

7. My mother and I

8. What gets me into trouble is

9. Education

10. When people are helpless

11. Women are lucky because

12. A good father

13. A girl has a right to

14. When they talked about sex, I

15. A wife should

16. I feel sorry

17. A man feels good when

18. Rules are

(Form 81 for Women)

Name_____

19. Crime and delinquency could be halted if

20. Men are lucky because

21. I just can't stand people who

22. At times she worried about

23. I am

24. A woman feels good when

25. My main problem is

26. A husband has a right to

27. The worst thing about being a woman

28. A good mother

29. When I am with a man

30. Sometimes she wished that

31. My father

32. If I can't get what I want

33. Usually she felt that sex

34. For a woman a career is

35. My conscience bothers me if

36. A woman should always

SENTENCE COMPLETION FOR MEN (Form 81)

Name_____Age____Marital Status____Education_____

Instructions: Complete the following sentences.

1. When a child will not join in group activities

2. Raising a family

3. When I am criticized

4. A man's job

5. Being with other people

6. The thing I like about myself is

7. My mother and I

8. What gets me into trouble is

9. Education

10. When people are helpless

11. Women are lucky because

12. A good father

13. A girl has a right to

14. When they talked about sex, I

15. A wife should

16. I feel sorry

17. A man feels good when

18. Rules are

(Form 81 for Men)

Name_____

19. Crime and delinquency could be halted if

20. Men are lucky because

21. I just can't stand people who

22. At times he worried about

23. I am

24. A woman feels good when

25. My main problem is

26. A husband has a right to

27. The worst thing about being a man

28. A good mother

29. When I am with a woman

30. Sometimes he wished that

31. My father

32. If I can't get what I want

33. Usually he felt that sex

34. For a woman a career is

35. My conscience bothers me if

36. A man should always

SENTENCE COMPLETION FOR WOMEN (*Form 11-68*)

Name _____ Age _____

Marital Status _____ Education _____

Instructions: Complete the following sentences.

1. Raising a family
2. A girl has a right to
3. When they avoided me
4. If my mother
5. Being with other people
6. The thing I like about myself is
7. My mother and I
8. What gets me into trouble is
9. Education
10. When people are helpless
11. Women are lucky because
12. My father
13. A pregnant woman
14. When my mother spanked me, I
15. A wife should
16. I feel sorry
17. Rules are
18. When I get mad
19. When a child will not join in group activities
20. Men are lucky because
21. When they talked about sex, I
22. At times she worried about
23. I am
24. A woman feels good when
25. My main problem is
26. My husband and I will
27. The worst thing about being a woman
28. A good mother
29. Sometimes she wished that
30. When I am with a man
31. When she thought of her mother, she
32. If I can't get what I want
33. Usually she felt that sex
34. For a woman a career is
35. My conscience bothers me if
36. A woman should always

SENTENCE COMPLETION FOR MEN (*Form 11-68*)

Name .... Age ....

Marital Status .... Education ....

Instructions: Complete the following sentences.

1. Raising a family
2. When a child will not join in group activities
3. When they avoided me
4. A man's job
5. Being with other people
6. The thing I like about myself is
7. If my mother
8. Crime and delinquency could be halted if
9. When I am with a woman
10. Education
11. When people are helpless
12. Women are lucky because
13. What gets me into trouble is
14. A good father
15. A man feels good when
16. A wife should
17. I feel sorry
18. A man should always
19. Rules are
20. When they talked about sex, I
21. Men are lucky because
22. My father and I
23. When his wife asked him to help with the housework
24. Usually he felt that sex
25. At times he worried about
26. If I can't get what I want
27. My main problem is
28. When I am criticized
29. Sometimes he wished that
30. A husband has a right to
31. When he thought of his mother, he
32. The worst thing about being a man
33. If I had more money
34. I just can't stand people who
35. My conscience bothers me if
36. He felt proud that he

SENTENCE COMPLETION FOR WOMEN (*Form 9-62*)

Name .... Age ....

Marital Status .... Education ....

Instructions: Complete the following sentences.

1. Raising a family
2. Most men think that women
3. When they avoided me
4. If my mother
5. Being with other people
6. The thing I like about myself is
7. My mother and I
8. What gets me into trouble is
9. Education
10. When people are helpless
11. Women are lucky because
12. My father
13. A pregnant woman
14. When my mother spanked me, I
15. A wife should
16. I feel sorry
17. When I am nervous, I
18. A woman's body
19. When a child won't join in group activities

20. Men are lucky because
21. When they talked about sex, I
22. At times she worried about
23. I am
24. A woman feels good when
25. My main problem is
26. Whenever she was with her mother, she
27. The worst thing about being a woman
28. A good mother
29. Sometimes she wished that
30. When I am with a man
31. When she thought of her mother, she
32. If I can't get what I want
33. Usually she felt that sex
34. For a woman a career is
35. My conscience bothers me if
36. A woman should always

SENTENCE COMPLETION FOR MEN (*Form 9-62*)

Name .... Age ....

Marital Status .... Education ....

Instructions: Complete the following sentences.

1. Raising a family
2. Most women think that men
3. When they avoided me
4. If my mother
5. Being with other people
6. The thing I like about myself is
7. A man's job
8. If I can't get what I want
9. I am embarrassed when
10. Education
11. When people are helpless
12. Women are lucky because
13. What gets me into trouble is
14. A good father
15. If I were king
16. A wife should
17. I feel sorry
18. When a child won't join in group activities
19. When I am nervous, I

20. He felt proud that he
21. Men are lucky because
22. When they talked about sex, I
23. At times he worried about
24. I am
25. A man feels good when
26. My main problem is
27. When his wife asked him to help with the housework
28. When I am criticized
29. Sometimes he wished that
30. When I am with a woman
31. When he thought of his mother, he
32. The worst thing about being a man
33. Usually he felt that sex
34. I just can't stand people who
35. My conscience bothers me if
36. Crime and delinquency could be halted if

SENTENCE COMPLETION FOR BOYS (FORM 2-77)

NAME_____SCHOOL_____AGE_____

DATE_____TEACHER_____BIRTHDATE_____

INSTRUCTIONS: Complete the following sentences in any way that you wish.

1. If I had more money

2. A man's job

3. When a child will not join in group activities

4. My father and I

5. The thing I like about myself is

6. Being with other people

7. If my mother

8. Education

9. What gets me into trouble is

10. A good father

(FORM 2-77 BOYS)

NAME_____

11. I feel sorry

12. The worst thing about being a man

13. Women are lucky because

14. At times he worried about

15. He felt proud that he

16. Rules are

17. When he thought of his mother, he

18. When I get mad

19. When they avoided me

20. Raising a family

21. I am

22. A husband has a right to

23. I just can't stand people who

(FORM 2-77 BOYS)

NAME_____

24. My father

25. If I can't get what I want

26. A boy feels good when

27. My main problem is

28. Crime and delinquency could be halted if

29. Sometimes he wished that

30. When I am criticized

31. If I were king

32. When people are helpless

33. When my mother spanked me, I

34. Men are lucky because

35. My conscience bothers me if

36. A man should always

SENTENCE COMPLETION FOR GIRLS (FORM 2-77)

NAME_____ SCHOOL_____ AGE_____

DATE_____ TEACHER_____ BIRTHDATE_____

INSTRUCTIONS: Complete the following sentences in any way that you wish.

1. If I had more money

2. A wife should

3. When a child will not join in group activities

4. My mother and I

5. The thing I like about myself is

6. Being with other people

7. If my mother

8. Education

9. What gets me into trouble is

10. A good mother

(FORM 2-77 GIRLS)

NAME_____

11. I feel sorry

12. The worst thing about being a woman

13. Women are lucky because

14. At times she worried about

15. She felt proud that she

16. Rules are

17. When she thought of her mother, she

18. When I get mad

19. When they avoided me

20. Raising a family

21. I am

22. A girl has a right to

23. I just can't stand people who

NAME_____

24. My father

25. If I can't get what I want

26. A girl feels good when

27. My main problem is

28. Crime and delinquency could be halted if

29. Sometimes she wished that

30. When I am criticized

31. If I were king

32. When people are helpless

33. When my mother spanked me, I

34. Men are lucky because

35. My conscience bothers me if

36. A woman should always

Appendix D
Excel Macros for Handling SCT Data

The following macros have been tested with Excel 5 and Excel for Windows 95.

```
'
' Prepare Macro *** Setting up the columns in the spreadsheet.
'
Sub A_Prepare()
    ' Entering column headings.
    Range("A1").Formula = "Sex"
    Range("B1").Formula = "ID"
    Range("C1").Formula = "Item"
    Range("D1").Formula = "E1"
    Range("E1").Formula = "C1"
    Range("F1").Formula = "E2"
    Range("G1").Formula = "C2"
    Range("H1").Formula = "EF"
    Range("I1").Formula = "Response1"
    Range("J1").Formula = "Response2"
    Range("K1").Formula = "Ogive"
    Range("L1").Formula = "TPR/Sum"
    ' Setting column width.
    Columns("A:C").ColumnWidth = 3
    Columns("D:K").ColumnWidth = 2
    Columns("I:I").ColumnWidth = 45
End Sub
'
' Stems Macro *** Entering 36 Stems and Stem numbers, with ID=0.
'
Sub B_Stems()
    ' Giving the stems an ID of 0
    Range("B2").Select
    ActiveCell.Formula = "0"
    ActiveCell.AutoFill
```

Destination:=ActiveCell.Range("A1:A36")
' Typing in stem numbers from 1 to 36
Range("C2").Select
ActiveCell.Formula = "1"
ActiveCell.AutoFill
Destination:=ActiveCell.Range("A1:A36"), Type:=xlLinearTrend
' Typing in the 36 stems
Range("I2").Formula =
"   Item 1. When a child will not join in group activities"
Range("I3").Formula = " Item 2. Raising a family"
Range("I4").Formula = " Item 3. When I am criticized"
Range("I5").Formula = " Item 4. A man's job"
Range("I6").Formula = " Item 5. Being with other people"
Range("I7").Formula = " Item 6. The thing I like about myself is"
Range("I8").Formula = " Item 7. My mother and I"
Range("I9").Formula = " Item 8. What gets me into trouble is"
Range("I10").Formula = " Item 9. Education"
Range("I11").Formula = " Item 10. When people are helpless"
Range("I12").Formula = " Item 11. Women are lucky because"
Range("I13").Formula = " Item 12. A good father"
Range("I14").Formula = " Item 13. A girl has a right to"
Range("I15").Formula = " Item 14. When they talked about sex, I"
Range("I16").Formula = " Item 15. A wife should"
Range("I17").Formula = " Item 16. I feel sorry"
Range("I18").Formula = " Item 17. A man feels good when"
Range("I19").Formula = " Item 18. Rules are"
Range("I20").Formula =
"   Item 19. Crime and delinquency could be halted if"
Range("I21").Formula = " Item 20. Men are lucky because"
Range("I22").Formula = " Item 21. I just can't stand people who"
Range("I23").Formula = " Item 22. At times she (he) worries about"
Range("I24").Formula = " Item 23. I am"
Range("I25").Formula = " Item 24. A woman feels good when"
Range("I26").Formula = " Item 25. My main problem is"
Range("I27").Formula = " Item 26. A husband has a right to"
Range("I28").Formula =
"   Item 27. The worst thing about being a woman (man)"
Range("I29").Formula = " Item 28. A good mother"
Range("I30").Formula = " Item 29. When I am with a man (woman)"
Range("I31").Formula = " Item 30. Sometimes she (he) wished that"
Range("I32").Formula = " Item 31. My father"
Range("I33").Formula = " Item 32. If I can't get what I want"

```
        Range("I34").Formula = "  Item 33. Usually she (he) feels that sex"
        Range("I35").Formula = "  Item 34. For a woman a career is"
        Range("I36").Formula = "  Item 35. My conscience bothers me if"
        Range("I37").Formula = "  Item 36. A woman (man) should always"
        ' Moving the cursor to the first protocol
        Range("A38").Select
End Sub
'
' Protocol Macro*** Repeating sex & ID to the next 35 lines,
'                  ***  and adding 36 item numbers for each  protocol.
'                  *** Remember to type in sex and ID before running this macro
'                  ***  and put the cursor in the cell to the right of the ID,
'                  ***  in the "item" column of the first response.
'

Sub C_Protocol()
        ' Filling in 36 item numbers.
        ActiveCell.Formula = "1"
        ActiveCell.AutoFill
            Destination:=ActiveCell.Range("A1:A36"), Type:=xlLinearTrend
        ActiveCell.Offset(0, -2).Range("A1:B36").FillDown
        ' Moving the cursor to the response column.
        ' Type in the responses before typing in the sex and ID of the  next protocol.
        ActiveCell.Offset(0, 6).Select
End Sub
'
' D_IRL Macro  *** Sorting into the Item Response Lists
'              *** (by item number & response)
Sub IRL()
        Cells.Select
        Selection.Sort Key1:=Columns("C"), Key2:=Columns("I"),_
            Header:=xlYes
End Sub
'
' SortID Macro*** Sorting the worksheet by ID and Item number ***
'
Sub SortID()
        Cells.Select
        Selection.Sort Key1:=Columns("B"), Key2:=Columns("C"),_
            Header:=xlYes
End Sub
'
' TPR Macro*** Generating TPRs for each protocol.
```

```
'
                *** The cursor must be at the final rating of the response Item 1.
'
Sub TPR()
    ' Copying the ratings to the Ogive column, then sorting in descending order
    ' to prepare for the calculations later
    ActiveCell.Range("A1:A36").Copy
    ActiveCell.Offset(0, 3).Range("A1:A36").Select
    Selection.PasteSpecial Paste:=xlValues
    Selection.Sort Key1:=ActiveCell, Order1:=xlDescending
    ' Typing the headings for the three calculations
    ActiveCell.Offset(0, 2).Formula = "Ogive TPR"
    ActiveCell.Offset(1, 2).Formula = "Item Sum TPR"
    ActiveCell.Offset(2, 2).Formula = "Item Sum"
    ' Calculating the Ogive TPR. The whole IF statement must be on one line.
    ActiveCell.Offset(0, 1).Select
    ActiveCell.Formula = _
        "=IF(R[1]C[-1] > 8,""E9"",IF(R[4]C[-1] > 7,""E8"",IF(R[5]C[-
        -1]>6,""E7"",IF(R[11]C[-1]>5,""E6"",IF(R[15]C[-1]-
        4,""E5"",IF(R[31]C[-1]<,""E2"",IF(R[30]C[-1]<4,""E3"",""E4"")))))))"
    ' Calculating the Item Sum value
    ActiveCell.Offset(1, 0).Formula = _
        "=SUM(R[-1]C[-1]:R[34]C[-1])"
    ' Calculating the Item Sum TPR.
    ' The whole IF statement must be on one line.
    ActiveCell.Offset(2, 0).Formula = _
        "=IF(R[-1]C>234,""E9"",IF(R[-1]C>216,""E8"",IF(R[-
        -1]C>200,""E7"",IF(R[-1]C>180,""E6"",IF(R[-1]C>162,""E5"",IF(R-
        R[-1]C< 133,""E2"",IF(R[-1]C < 146,""E3"",""E4"")))))))"
    ' Moving the curser to the next protocol, to be rated by the TPR macro.
    ActiveCell.Offset(36, -4).Select
End Sub
```

Inquiries concerning the macro may be addressed to:
http://members.aol.com/cmhs 2000/staff/hy/sctmacro.html

Appendix E
Rule for Locating Categories

Kathryn Bobbitt
Private Practice, Waverly, WV
Lê Xuân Hy
Center for Multicultural Human Services
Jane Loevinger
Washington University

A category i is located at level Ek when both of the following conditions are met:

1. The probability that a person who has a TPR at or below level Ek will give a response in category i exceeds the probability that a person with TPR above level Ek will give a response in category i.
2. The probability that a person who has a TPR at or above Ek gives a response in category i exceeds the probability that a person with TPR below Ek will do so.

The probability that a person with given TPR Ej will give a response in category i is n_{ij}/N_j, where N_j is the number in the sample at level j, and n_{ij} is the number in category i at level j, that is, with a TPR of Ej. (Ej goes from E2 to E9.)

$$1.\ \sum_{2}^{k} n_{ij}/N_j > \sum_{k+1}^{9} n_{ij}/Nj$$

$$2.\ \sum_{2}^{k-1} n_{ij}/N_j < \sum_{k}^{9} n_{ij}/Nj$$

The rule is not helpful at extreme ratings. However, the number of cases per category at the extremes is so small that theory or intuition is a more reliable guide.

A single response given by a person with an extreme TPR will be too heavily weighted if there are few cases in the base rates at that level and the number of cases in the category is small. If the data are entered into a spreadsheet, one can easily try out what difference it would have made if that case had had a TPR of, say, E-7 instead of E-8. On this basis, the rule may be overruled.

Appendix F
How to Use the SCT in Translation

Lê Xuân Hy
Center for Multicultural Human Services

Responding to the stem "A man should always—" a young boy wrote in Vietnamese, "*nhan, nghia, le, tri, tin*" which means "[be] benevolent, just, civil, knowledgeable, trustworthy." Such a combination of different and complementary virtues suggests a high rating. The boy was quoting a popular saying by Confucius, memorized by many grade school students in Vietnam. It is likely that he could not explain any of the five classical, Chinese-rooted words in that saying. Had there been an empirical Vietnamese manual, that response probably would be identified as a cliché to be rated at about E4.

Using tests in translation has many such problems. The SCT is particularly sensitive to language. For the stem "When people are helpless—," for example, the response "—they need help" is at E4 but "—they need someone to help them" is at E5. Such small differences may be lost in translation.

This appendix neither lists nor discusses all problems with using a translated test. Instead, it provides some suggestions to avoid or minimize some of the problems. These suggestions are not the only ones, but they have been tested and work reasonably well. They take time, but without them or some similarly time-consuming and thought-out procedures, systematic errors are likely to increase.

If the raters do not know the other language, both the stems and the responses need to be translated. There are only 36 short stems to translate, but translating them is more difficult than translating the responses.

TRANSLATING THE STEMS

The ideal translated stems should (a) be understandable by people from a wide range of educational backgrounds; (b) have both the meaning and the ambiguity of the stems, so that the full range of topics in the rating manual are available to the test takers; and (c) not have a higher or lower pull, compared to the original stems.

Some of these qualities, such as the high or low pull, must be tested by empirical research. Careful translation, on the other hand, can lead to some of these desirable characteristics.

Translations come from translators. One commonly used but poor type of translators is the foreign student in an English-speaking university. The fact that the students perform well in English may mean that they have spent so much time in an English-speaking environment that their development in the first language might have been arrested. These students can produce translations that are so close to English in both grammar and pragmatics that their backward translation would match perfectly with the original. Thus, the common and useful method of backward translation cannot serve as the only quality check.

Another commonly used type of translator is the community leader who may use such a learned language that some people cannot understand. The professional translator also has another set of problems that have been discussed in various articles. The method that has worked for us is an iterative process with the following steps:

- Identify the population to be studied, and the particular type of language that group uses. For example, Spanish for Cubans born in the United States versus Spanish for Cubans in Cuba versus Spanish for Spaniards.
- From the particular language group, identify several translators who are fluent in English and function actively in the other language. If the principal investigator does not know the other language, it is difficult for him or her to judge the fluency of the translators in that language. Thus, active participation in the language community is used as a proxy measure of fluency. Daily home use of the other language is a desirable characteristic but not sufficient because that home might be isolated and its language peculiar. Participation in a larger group, such as a youth group or a church group, is also necessary. Recommendations from that community are also useful.
- Give the SCT in English to two or three of the translators. Their responses can give one indication of how they understand the test, and the experience of taking the test also helps them understand the test better.
- Ask each of them to translate the test independently.
- Compare and discuss their translations in light of the three desirable characteristics of the translation just described. They need to look at the themes of items, as well as the lowest and highest responses in the rating manual. Although there are only a few themes per item, and few responses at the lowest and highest levels, going through each of the items takes much time.
- Arrive at the first translation. Proper focus group techniques can help to ensure that no one person influences the translation by his or her forcefulness, rank,

or other factors. In a group of Asians, for example, an older person may have more respect and thus his or her translation may have more influence on the group, but if the population to be studied are young students that influence would be inappropriate.

- Ask two or three other translators to take the translated test, then ask them to translate both the items and their responses back to English independently.
- Review their responses to see whether they are ratable by the manual. If a substantial number of their responses are too unique for the rating manual to be useful, then either the translation of the stems has to be improved or the test requires an empirical rating manual in that language.
- Ask each of them independently what they think each stem means and what are the possible responses people might have.
- Discuss differences among their backward translations, and between the original English version and the backward-translation version. Inform these translators that the goal is an effective translation, not a better backward translation. Arrive at improvements of the translation.
- If significant improvements are made, the new version will need to be tested again with a new group of several translators, going through the process of taking the test, translating the items and the responses, checking the ratability of the responses, discussing the possible meanings of the stems and the backward translations, which may result in further changes. Independence (working with each person privately) and proper focus group techniques (when the translators work together) are important.
- In addition, a consultant with both linguistic and testing background would be useful throughout the process.

After two or three rounds, a consensus should build up for the translation of most items. A few items may not have an ideal translation. Note on how that translation might differ from the original in English should be recorded for future raters.

The process still requires pilot testing as usual. The responses from the pilot testing should be translated and rated. There might be surprises partly because the actual respondents are probably monolingual, thus differ significantly from the bilingual translators. Responses should be examined for ratability, internal consistency, and correlations with other variables. For example, had the response from Confucius given the young boy a high rating for that item, the internal consistency in the protocol would be low.

No matter how careful the translation is, the translated stems may differ from the original. For example, some languages are relational, so the translation of the word "I" would differ according to the testing situation, as described in chapter 7. One can argue, however, that a perfect translation is desirable but not necessary. In the process of constructing the test, experienced raters rated new items using guidance from theory and experience from other items. Thus, as long as the differences between the original and the translated items are explicit, experienced raters should do well.

TRANSLATING THE RESPONSES

Some responses may be more difficult to translate than the simple stems, but each error is not as weighty as an error in translating a stem. Some problems are not unique to the SCT in translation, such as illegible script or ambiguous statements. If there is doubt, the translators, functioning like interpreters, should attach a note to the raters. The note can cover such semantic and pragmatic issues as the following:

- Ambiguous responses: provide both possible meanings.
- Expressions not understandable in English: provide the literal translation and attach an interpretation including both the meaning and the usage.
- Expressions understandable in English but have a different usage, such as clichés.

In a large project, there may be several translators or one translator working over a long period during which consistency across persons and within person across time may become an issue. Thus all translation notes (of both stems and responses) should be kept in one place and reviewed regularly by all translators in order to assure reliability.

TRAINING RATERS

The standard rating procedure requires two raters for every response. If only one rater can read the other language, he or she may have a tacit knowledge that influences the final ratings. Ideally, this tacit knowledge should become explicit to such an extent that over a short period of time the other rater can achieve almost the same level of accuracy. One procedure follows:

The two raters start with the pilot data or a small subsample, rating items independently and then discussing their ratings. All questions and discussions between the two raters are in writing. The recent popularity of e-mail now simplifies this task. Interrater reliability, correlations between each rater and the final scores, and mean differences between each rater and the final scores are calculated to see who has more influence on the final scores. It is likely that in the first sample, the rater with knowledge of the other language would have a rating closer to the final scores.

The process is repeated with another small subsample, and repeated again if necessary, until the two raters contribute equally to the final scores, taking their rating experience into account.

Although the processes just described are time-consuming, they are still easier, and not as valuable as creating a new manual in the other language and then studying the equivalence between the two tests, as Westenberg, Jonckheer, Treffers, and Drewes (1998) have done in Dutch.

ACKNOWLEDGMENTS

I thank Michiel Westenberg, Vicki Carlson, Doyle Cozadd, and Brian Van Hove for their valuable feedback and corrections.

References

Adorno, T. W., Frenkel-Brunswik, E., Levinson, D. J., & Sanford, R. N. (1950). *The authoritarian personality.* New York: Harper & Row.

Arredondo, P.M. (1984). Identity themes for immigrant young adults. *Adolescence, 19,* 977-993.

Arredondo-Dowd, P.M. (1981). The psychological development and education of immigrant adolescents: A baseline study. *Adolescence, 16,* 175-186.

Blasi, A. (1971). *A developmental approach to responsibility training.* Unpublished doctoral dissertation, Washington University, St. Louis, MO

Blasi, A. (1976).Personal responsibility and ego development. In R. deCharms (Ed.), *Enhancing motivation: Change in the classroom.* New York: Irvington.

Blasi, A. (1984). *Autonomie im Gehorsam:Die Entwicklung des Distanzierungsvermögens im socialisierten Handeln* [Autonomy in obedience: The development of distancing in socialized action]. In W. Edelstein & J. Habermas (Eds.), *Soziale Interaktion und sociales Verstehen* (pp. 300-347). Frankfurt am Main: Suhrkamp.

Blasi, A. (1997). Loevinger's theory of ego development and its relations to the cognitive-developmental approach, In P. M. Westenberg, A. Blasi, & L. D. Cohn (Eds.), *Personality development: Theoretical, empirical, and clinical analyses of Loevinger's conception of ego development.* Mahwah, NJ: Lawrence Erlbaum Associates.

Blumentritt, T., Novy, D. M., Gaa, J. P., & Liberman, D. (1996). Effects of maximum performance instructions on the Sentence Completion Test of Ego Development. *Journal of Personality Assessment, 67,* 79-89.

Colby, A., & Kohlberg, L. (1987). *The measurement of moral judgment.* Cambridge, England: Cambridge University Press.

Cole, M. (1996). *Cultural psychology.* Cambridge, MA: Harvard University Press.

Costa, M. E., & Campos, B. P. (1987). Area de estudos universitarios e densenvolvimento do ego [University area of study and ego development of students]. *Codernos de Consulta Psicologica, 3,* 5-11.

Dhruvarajan, V. (1981). *Level of self differentiation: Caste status vs. mundane experience.* Unpublished doctoral dissertation, Department of Sociology, University of Chicago, Chicago, IL.

Dunston, P. J., & Roberts, A. (1987). The relationship of moral judgement and ego development to political-social values in Black college students. *The Journal of Black Psychology, 13,* 43-49.

Frank, S., & Quinlan, D. M. (1976). Ego development and female delinquency: A cognitive-developmental approach. *Journal of Abnormal Psychology , 85,* 505-510.

Haan, N., & Stroud, J. (1973). Moral and ego stages in relationship to ego processes: A study of "hippies." *Journal of Personality, 41,* 596-612.

Hall, C. C. (1997). Cultural malpractice: The growing obsolescence of psychology with the changing U.S. population, *American Psychologist, 52*, 642-651.

Hauser, S. T. (1976). Loevinger's model and measure of ego development: A critical review. *Psychological Bulletin, 83*, 928-995.

Hauser, S. T., Powers, S. I, & Noam, G. G. (1991). *Adolescents and their families: Paths of ego development.* New York: The Free Press.

Heath, D. H. (1968). *Growing up in college.* San Francisco: Jossey-Bass.

Holt, R. R. (1980). Loevinger's measure of ego development: Reliability and national norms for male and female short forms. *Journal of Personality and Social Psychology, 39*, 909-920.

Hy, L. X. (1986). *Cross-cultural measurement of ego development: Responses in different languages.* Unpublished doctoral dissertation, Washington University, St. Louis, MO.

Hy, L. X., & Bobbitt, K. H. (1991). *Ego development theory and methods: A review of developmental levels, test forms, and scoring rules.* Manuscript submitted for publication.

Hy, L. X., & Loevinger, J. (1989). *Measuring ego development: Supplementary manual and exercises for Form 81 of the WUSCT.*

Hy, L. X. & Loevinger, J. (1996). *Measuring ego development* (2nd ed.). Mahwah, NJ: Lawrence Erlbaum Associates.

Isaacs, K. S. (1956). *Relatability, a proposed construct and an approach to its validation.* Unpublished doctoral dissertation, University of Chicago, Chicago, IL.

Kapfhammer, H.P., Neumeier, R., & Scherer, J. (1993). Ich-Entwicklung im Ubergang von Jugend und jungem Erwachsenenalter: Eine empirische Vergleichsstudie bei psychiatrischen patienten und gesunden Kontrollprobanden [Ego development in the transition from youth and young adulthood: An empirical comparison study of patients and healthy controls]. *Praxis der kinderpsychologie and kinderpsychiatric, 42*, 106-113.

Kato, (1981). *Investigation of personal development in the adolescent period by the Sentence Completion Method.* Paper presented at the 23rd annual meeting of the Japanese Association of Educational Psychology.

Kohlberg, L. (1969). Stage and sequence: The cognitive-developmental approach to socialization. In D. A. Goslin (Ed.) *Handbook of socialization theory and research* (pp. 347-480).

Kusatsu, O. (1977). Ego development and socio-cultural process in Japan. *I. Keizagaku-Kiyp, 3*, 41-109.

Kusatsu, O. (1978). Ego development and socio-cultural process in Japan, II *I. Keizagaku-Kiyp, __* , 74-128.

Lambert, H. V. (1972) *A comparison of Jane Loevinger's theory of ego development and Lawrence Kohlberg's theory of moral development.* Unpublished doctoral dissertation, University of Chicago, Chicago, IL.

Lasker, H. M. (1977). *Interim summative evaluation report: An initial assessment of the Shell/Humanas OD program.* Cambridge, MA: Harvard University Press.

Lasker, H. M. (1978). *Ego development and motivation: A cross-cultural cognitive-developmental analysis of n achievement.* Unpublished doctoral dissertation, University of Chicago, Chicago, IL.

Limoges, J. (1979). *The effects of students' development of a conceptual approach to career education.* Unpublished doctoral dissertation, Boston University, Boston, MA.

Limoges, J. (1980). Quand l'orientation devient "egologique." *Revue des sciences de l'education, 1*, 34-49.

Loevinger, J. (1953) The mother-blaming complex among psychologists. *American Psychologist, 8*, 748-750.

Loevinger, J. (1976). *Ego development: Conceptions and theories.* San Francisco: Jossey-Bass.

Loevinger, J. (1979). Construct validity of the sentence completion test for ego development. *Applied Psychological Measurement, 3*, 291-311.

Loevinger, J. (1985). Revision of the Sentence Completion Test for ego development. *Journal of Personality and Social Psychology, 48*, 420-427.

Loevinger, J. (1993a). Ego development: Questions of method and theory. *Psychological Inquiry, 4*, 56-63.

Loevinger, J. (1993b). Measurement of personality: True or false. *Psychological Inquiry, 4*, 1-16.

Loevinger, J., Gleser, G. C., & DuBois, P. H. (1953). Maximizing the discriminating power of a multiple-score test. *Psychometrika, 18*, 309-317.

Loevinger, J., Sweet, B., Ossorio, A., & LaPerriere, K. (1962). Measuring personality patterns of women. *Genetic Psychology Monographs, 65*, 53-136.

Loevinger, J., & Wessler, R. (1970). *Measuring ego development. 1. Construction and use of a sentence completion test.* San Francisco: Jossey-Bass.

Loevinger, J., Wessler, R., & Redmore, C. D. (1970). *Measuring ego development. 2. Scoring manual for women and girls.* San Francisco: Jossey-Bass.

Looney, J. (1988). Ego development and black identity. *The Journal of Black Psychology, 15,* 41-56.

Luborsky, L. (1953). Self-interpretation of the TAT as a clinical technique. *Journal of Personality Assessment and Projective Techniques, 17,* 217-223.

Maslow, A. (1954). *Motivation and personality.* New York: Harper.

McCammon, E. P. (1981). Comparison of oral and written forms of the Sentence Completion Test for ego development. *Developmental Psychology, 39,* 233-235.

McCrae, R. R., & Costa, P. T., Jr. (1980). Openness to experience and ego level in Loevinger's Sentence Completion Test: Dispositional contributions to developmental models of personality. *Journal of Personality and Social Psychology, 39,* 1179-1190.

McCrae, R. R., & Costa, P. T. (1997). Personality trait structure as a human universal, *American Psychologist, 52,* 509-516.

Mikel, E. (1974). *Preliminary research studies of character development among imprisoned offenders.* Unpublished manuscript, Washington University, St. Louis, MO.

Mosher, R. L., & Sprinthal, N. A. (1971). Psychological education: A means to promote personal development during adolescence. *Counseling Psychologist, 2,* 3-82.

Miyashita, K., & Uechi, Y. (1981). Loevinger's ego development theory - summary and induction of it to our country. *Hiroshima University Education Department, 1*(30), 225-235.

Miyashita, K., & Uechi, Y. (1983). Loevinger's ego development theory — an investigation of its reliability and validity. *Hiroshima University Education Department, 1*(31), 207-211.

Nettles, E. J., & Loevinger, J. (1983). Sex role expectations and ego level in relation to problem marriages. *Journal of Personality and Social Psychology, 43,* 676-687.

Novy, D. M. (1992). Gender comparability of forms 81 of the Washington University Sentence Completion Test. *Educational and Psychological Measurement, 52,* 491-497.

Novy, D. M. (1993). An investigation of the progressive sequence of ego development levels. *Journal of Clinical Psychology, 49,* 332-338.

Novy, D. M., & Francis, D. J. (1992). Psychometric properties of the Washington University Sentence Completion Test. *Educational & Psychological Measurement, 52,* 1029-1039.

Paul, D. (1979). *The effects of interpersonal process recall on the responsibility level and the frequency of counseling activities of community health nurses.* Unpublished doctoral dissertation, Boston University, Boston, MA.

Paul, D. (1980). La théorie du développement de l'ego et son utilité pour la profession [The theory of ego development and its usefulness for the profession]. *L'infirmière Canadienne,* 22-25.

Powitzky, R. J. (1975). *Ego level and types of federal offenses.* Unpublished doctoral dissertation, University of Texas Health Science Center, Dallas.

Ravinder, S. (1986). Loevinger's Sentence Completion Test of ego development: A useful tool for cross-cultural researchers. *International Journal of Psychology, 21,* 679-684.

Redmore, C. (1976). Susceptibility to faking of a sentence completion test of ego development. *Journal of Personality Assessment, 40,* 607-616.

Redmore, C. D., & Loevinger, J. (1979). Ego development in adolescence: Longitudinal studies. *Journal of youth and adolescence, 8,* 1-20.

Redmore, C. D., Loevinger, J., Tamashiro, R. (1978-1981). *Measuring ego development, Scoring manual for men and boys* (mimeographed). Washington University, St. Louis, MO.

Redmore, C., & Waldman, K. (1975). Reliability of a sentence completion measure of ego development. *Journal of Personality Assessment, 39,* 236-243.

Rock, M. (1975). *Self-reflection and ego development.* Unpublished doctoral dissertation, New York University, New York.

Rogers, A. G. (1987). *Gender differences in moral reasoning: A validity study of two moral orientations.* Unpublished doctoral dissertation, Washington University, Saint Louis, MO.

Sasaki, M. (1980). Loevinger's measurement technique of ego development and recent studies based on it. *Japanese Psychological Review, 23*(4), 392-414.

Sasaki, M. (1981a). Measuring ego development of female adolescents by sentence completions. *The Japanese Journal of Educational Psychology, 29,* 147-151.

Sasaki, M. (1981b). Ego development of adult males. *Educational Counseling Journal of Tokyo University, 4*, 131-137.

Schaefer, E. S., & Bell, R. Q. (1958). Development of a parental attitude research instrument. *Child Development, 29*, 339-361.

Sears, R. R., Maccoby, E. E., & Levin, H. (1957). *Patterns of child rearing*. Evanston, IL: Row, Peterson.

Shoben, E. J., Jr. (1949). The assessment of parental attitudes in relation to child adjustment. *Psychological Monographs, 39*, 101-148.

Snarey, J. R. (1985). Cross-cultural universality of social-moral development: A critical review of Kohlbergian research. *Psychological Bulletin , 97*, 202-232.

Snarey, J., & Blasi, J. (1980). Ego development among adult kibbutzniks: A cross-cultural application of Loevinger's theory. *Genetic Psychology Monographs, 102*, 117-157.

Sullivan, C., Grant, M. Q., & Grant, J. D. (1957). The development of interpersonal maturity: Applications to delinquency. *Psychiatry, 20*, 373-385.

Sullivan, E. V., McCullough, G., & Stager, M. A. (1970). A developmental study of the relationship between conceptual, ego, and moral development. *Child Development, 41*, 399-411.

Sullivan, H. S. (1953). *The interpersonal theory of psychiatry*. New York: Norton.

Suzman, R. (1974). The modernization of personality. *International Journal of Comparative Sociology, 14*, 273-287.

Tochio, J., & Akiba, H. (1988). Investigation on J. Loevinger's ego development—relation to female juvenile delinquents and their personality. *Osaka Education University, 37*, 17-27.

Tochio, J., & Hanada, C. (1991). Ego development of female delinquent adolescents: An examination based on Loevinger's theory. *Japanese Journal of Educational Psychologie, 39*, 324-331.

Vaillant, G. E., & McCullough, L. (1987). The Washington University Sentence Completion Test compared with other measures of adult ego development. *American Journal of Psychiatry, 144*, 1189-1194.

von der Lippe, A. (1988). Modre som modeller for dotres yrkesorientering [Mothers as models for occupational orientations in daughters]. *Tidsskrift for Norsk Psykologforening, 25*, 149-159.

Watanabe, M., & Yamamoto, R. (1989). Making a test of ego development using Sentence Completion Method: Translating and simplifying the Loevinger's WU-SCT. *Japanese Journal of Educational Psychology, 37*, 286-292.

Weathersby, R. (1993). Sri Lankan manager's leadership conceptualizations as a function of ego development. In J. Demick & P.M. Miller (Eds.), *Development in the workplace*. Hillsdale, NJ: Lawrence Erlbaum Associates.

Weiss, D. S., Zilberg, N. J., & Genevro, J. L. (1989). Psychometric properties of Loevinger's Sentence Completion Test in an adult psychiatric outpatient sample.

Westenberg, P. M., & Block, J. (1993). Ego development and individual differences in personality. *Journal of Personality and Social Psychology, 65*, 792-800.

Westenberg, P. M., Jonckheer, J., & Treffers, Ph. D. A. (in press). *Handleiding bij de Curium Zin Aanvul Test: Een Nederlandse Bewerking van de Washington University Sentence Completion Test for Ego Development]* [Manual for the Curium Sentence Completion Test: A Dutch Adaptation of the Washington University Sentence Comletion Test for Ego Development]. Lisse, The Netherlands: Swets Test Services.

Westenberg, P. M., Jonckheer, J., Treffers, Ph. D. A., & Drewes, M. J. (1998). Ego development in children and adolescents: Another side of the Impulsive, Self-protective, and Conformist ego levels. In P. M. Westenberg, A. Blasi, & L. D. Cohn (Eds.), *Personality development: Theoretical, empirical, and clinical investigations of Loevinger's conception of ego development*. Mahwah, NJ: Lawrence Erlbaum Associates.

Wurzman, I., Rounsaville, B. J., & Kleber, H. D. (1983). Cultural values of Puerto Rican opiate addicts: An exploratory study. *American Journal of Drug & Alcohol Abuse,9*, 141-153.

Zlotogorski, Z. (1985). Offspring of concentration camp survivors: A study of levels of ego functioning. *Israel Journal of Psychiatry and Related Sciences, 22*, 201-209.

Printed in the United States
139497LV00003B/6/P

9 780805 820591